P9-EDF-365

Women and Children First:

How to Avoid Crime

By Ken D. Biery, Jr., CPP

James L. Schaub, CPP

Other books and manuals by Ken D. Biery, Jr., CPP and James L. Schaub, CPP:

Physical Site Security Survey - Vision Press *
Computer Security Survey - Vision Press *
Financial Security Survey - Vision Press *

Law Enforcement, Security, and Fire Protection:
Career Paths, Successful Testing and Interviewing Techniques

- Win/Win Publications
(Release date November 1, 1992)

* Vision Press is a Canadian Publisher specializing in security related subjects.

Vision Press
#280 - 167 W. 2nd Avenue
Vancouver, B.C., Canada V5Y 1B8
Telephone (604) 873-3252
Fax (604) 873-3255

Win/Win Publications
© 1992 by Ken D. Biery, Jr. and James L. Schaub

Published in 1992 by

Win/Win Publications
P.O. Box 58125
Renton, Washington 98058
A division of CSC

Printed in the United States of America
10 9 8 7 6 5 4 3 2 1

Library of Congress Card Catalog Number 92-070988

ISBN: 1-881222-92-6

Editor: *Jaclyn Schaub*

Contributing Editors: *Stephen A. Schaub, Ph.D.*
                        Johnnie C. Crossler
                        Lynn McMurphy
                        Susan Edelblute

Illustrations: *James L. Schaub*, CPP

Photography: *Jaclyn Schaub*

ACKNOWLEDGMENT

We would like to thank the following individuals who have contributed time, effort, material, and dedication for no other reward than to see this project to its ultimate end — the possibility that a woman, child, or family will be saved the grief of becoming a victim. Without your help and support, this book would not have come to fruition.

Lynn McMurphy, Susan Edelblute, Stephen Schaub, Mary Schaub, Danielle Schaub, Johnnie C. Crossler, Randall S. Pettelle, Stuart M. Wagner, James Coleman, Stephanie Greenhouse, Sheila Pearce, Julie Afflerbach, Judy Logue and Cyndee Boyvey-Brown.

The authors would like to take this opportunity to extend a special thanks to Jaclyn Schaub. Jaclyn not only added emotional support throughout the investigative and writing phases of this book, but she also loaned her expertise as an editor, photographer, creative designer, and all around shoulder to cry on. Without you, this book would not be where it is today.

Jim
Ken

ABOUT THE AUTHORS

Ken D. Biery, Jr., CPP

Ken has been involved in security management roles within the hospitality industry for the past decade. Employed as a security manager for two major hotel chains. Ken's expertise has extended to the training of employees on personal safety issues, guest safety techniques, and VIP protection. He has educated security personnel in conflict mediation, "no-nonsense" self-defense, and physical security assessment. While Vice President of Corporate Security Consultants, Ken coauthored Physical Site Survey I, Computer Security Survey, and Financial Security Survey. Using his Communications degree, he has written articles on security training, terrorism, and physical security issues. Ken has provided in-depth security analysis for three National Park Service museums and historical park sites. Ken holds the prestigious designation of Certified Protection Professional (CPP) through the American Society for Industrial Security (ASIS). This highly respected designation is shared among only 3,000 security professionals throughout the world.

James L. Schaub, CPP

Jim Schaub has been involved in both law enforcement and Corporate Security for over one-third of his life. After having received a Bachelors of Science in Criminal Justice, Jim has been employed as a police officer, an investigator with a national company concerned with personnel and property protection and investigations, and aerospace security. In addition to his law enforcement experience and undergraduate education, his graduate level studies in the fields of family violence, judicial process, and juvenile delinquency have helped Jim develop an in-depth knowledge of criminal behavior.

As a Security Administrator in the information security department of The Boeing Company, Jim is currently responsible for the physical security of a multi-billion dollar military program. In conjunction with these responsibilities, he is also the President of Corporate Security Consultants and coauthor of Physical Site Survey I, Computer Security Survey, and Financial Security Survey. In their first month of publication, they sold internationally. He has authored a broad spectrum of security articles concerning such topics as: Physical Security, Security of Information Systems, Protection of Automated Information Systems Against Computer Virus Attacks. Jim also holds the prestigious Certified Protection Professional (CPP) designation from the American Society for Industrial Security.

TABLE OF CONTENTS

DISCLAIMER

This book was written for those interested in crime prevention and personal safety. It is sold with the understanding that the authors are only providing suggestions. Each situation has many variables; each person reacts differently and independently.

The authors shall in no way be held liable by any person, group of persons, or entity, with respect to any liability, loss, or damage, alleged or caused by, the information contained in this book.

This information is designed to complement and supplement other texts and crime prevention sources. For further information, see the references in the "Bibliography" and the "Additional Information" sections of this book.

The authors have spent hundreds of hours interviewing women and researching the information presented in this book. While every effort has been made to ensure the accuracy and completeness of this information, this book should only be used as a guide to crime prevention.

In today's world,

An ounce of prevention,

is worth a <u>TON</u> of cure.

NOTE TO THE READER

This book is formatted to present the necessary information to you in a short and concise manner. The format was deliberately chosen for this subject area. It has proven very effective for reading and retaining the information presented. The authors firmly believe that mental awareness is the key to avoiding most crimes.

"Women and Children: How To AVOID Crime," is designed for easy readability. It is intended to be carried with you. Hopefully after reading "Women and Children First: How to AVOID Crime," you will develop an awareness which will help you recognize and avoid crime and other potentially dangerous situations.

As you read this book, you will notice some redundancy of information. Many of the areas discussed throughout the book overlap. The authors prefer to mention information repeatedly to show its importance rather than presenting it once to save space.

WHY THIS BOOK NOW?

Late in July 1988, I received the call that all family members dread. My sister had been attacked! Three things struck me during this conversation. First, the attacker was on parole for multiple previous crimes — he had been incarcerated several times prior to this act. This was another example of an overburdened judicial system. Secondly, the astonishing fact that my sister talked the assailant out of actual penetrative rape! Thirdly, I remember the utter helplessness that I felt.

As a police officer, I had encountered many rapes, attacks, batterings and a multitude of other crimes. These happen in our homes and on our streets daily. I had always felt a deep personal loss when a member of our society was victimized by another. However, this incident acted as a crux, bringing all those atrocities in-line with what was now happening to my family.

Any victimization has a rippling effect. First, the victim is normally devastated. Whether this is personified by denial, hysteria, or coping with the situation; a change always occurs. Secondly, the family, friends, and loved ones of the victim become victims themselves. This may be personified by sympathy, reevaluation of their vulnerability, or by outright hate; they are touched too. In my case, I was one of the lucky "other victims." I had years of training to help cope with my family's victimization.

This book represents a personal promise to my sister and myself to help others avoid the experience which has touched too many U. S. citizens — the victims of crime. Luckily, I found another security professional, friend, and coauthor, Ken D. Biery, Jr., who shares my feelings. This book and its approach to crime avoidance is our contribution to all women — mothers, daughters, sisters, and their children.

While researching this book, one thing has become clear — IF YOU ARE VICTIMIZED, **IT IS NOT YOUR FAULT.** If a criminal is intent on raping you, or as a child you were victimized by an adult — **IT IS NOT YOUR FAULT.** After talking with hundreds of women, we have come to the conclusion that you can certainly take steps to avoid crime. However please realize, IF YOU ARE VICTIMIZED — **IT IS NOT YOUR FAULT.**

As I stated earlier, this book is a contribution to all those people who wish to AVOID crime. We have designed "*Women and Children First: How to AVOID Crime*" to be read in parts — to be one of those books that presents a difficult subject in an easy to read manner. Pick this book up, read a section; put it down, pick it up, read another. This is how the book was designed.

If one individual is spared the trauma of becoming a victim, then this book is a success. If you find this book has been useful to you, or you would like to add an avoidance technique of your own, please feel free to contact the authors. We can be contacted, care of:

Win/Win Publications
P.O. Box 58125
Renton, WA 98058

The Authors

      ⁻ *James L. Schaub, CPP*
      ⁻ *Ken D. Biery, Jr., CPP*

SITUATIONAL AWARENESS

Your mind is the single best weapon you possess. By being aware of how to avoid crime before it happens, you will reduce the opportunity for crime. If you are faced with a crime, this awareness may allow you to react quickly to the situation. The old cliche holds true where crime is concerned: An ounce of prevention is worth a pound of cure.

By being mentally aware, observant, and prepared, you will be able to deal with situations before, during, and after their occurrence. You need a daily rehearsal involving mental preparation using avoidance techniques for possible encounters with crime. This requires mentally picturing yourself identifying dangerous situations in your home, work place and recreational settings. This is the time to decide what you would do to avoid getting involved, and what actions you would take if you could not avoid the crime. Remember, the element of surprise is often a criminal's "best friend," so be sure to think about how you would react in those particular circumstances.

It is useful to look at how situational awareness can help you avoid crime. For example, you have been shopping at the mall one night. You notice an individual seems to be shopping in the same stores you are. He never looks at you directly or acknowledges your presence. You decide its a coincidence and leave the mall. It is a long, dark walk to your car and your mind is on the drive home. Suddenly, you feel a hand on your shoulder and then realize you are on the ground with someone holding you down. You are so surprised you cannot scream, move, or think. Although this scenario may not be avoided completely in real life, situational awareness could have helped you recognize the potential threat this individual posed. You could have requested a security escort to walk you to your car.

After awhile, recognition of potential criminal situations and avoidance will become as second nature as driving your car. While it may not always be pleasant, it really pays off, and the mental rehearsal is much better than the alternatives.

THE CRIMINAL MIND

It is important to remember that criminals will do and say anything to catch you off guard. Most criminals will relieve you of your possessions without a second thought. Many of these individuals would have "no problem" physically violating you in the process. Always question a person's motivation and how a situation appears. Naivete is charming, but not practical.

Criminals normally look for the easiest and quickest opportunities to succeed in their endeavors. They may employ techniques they learn from previous crimes or while in prison. Criminals may look like business professionals, college students, and even your next door neighbor. This is not to imply these people are criminals, but merely to illustrate there is no "look" or typical criminal profile.

☐ Always be aware of your environment. Above all, constantly be on the lookout for suspicious individuals and dangerous situations. Trust your instincts or gut feelings about people and situations. The best advice offered is to be AWARE! You do not have to be paranoid, but you should use your senses to be aware of both your actions and the environment surrounding you.

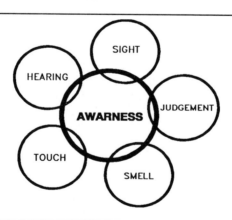

To AVOID crime, use all of your senses!

☐ Be mentally ready and constantly practice how to handle dangerous encounters. Make a habit of mentally rehearsing what you would do in a particular situation. Allowing fear to paralyze you may determine whether you will successfully escape an attacker or become the victim.

Preventive techniques, incorporated with an "awareness mind-set," will allow you to think clearly and act quickly. Many dangerous situations may simply be avoided if you develop personal protection awareness. These techniques are easy to use and can be triggered automatically without stimulating a paralyzing fear response.

Your local police department's crime prevention officers are an excellent resource for information on the prevention of crime and what victim services are available in your area. It is highly recommended that you find out about these resources **before you have to use them**.

VIOLENT CRIMES

The bad news is, within the United States, there is a VIOLENT crime committed approximately every twenty seconds. This statistic is broken down to one forcible rape reported every five minutes, one aggravated assault every thirty seconds, one robbery every forty-nine seconds, and an astounding one murder every twenty-two minutes.

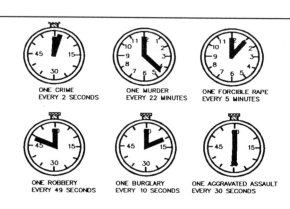

| ONE CRIME EVERY 2 SECONDS | ONE MURDER EVERY 22 MINUTES | ONE FORCIBLE RAPE EVERY 5 MINUTES |
| ONE ROBBERY EVERY 49 SECONDS | ONE BURGLARY EVERY 10 SECONDS | ONE AGGRAVATED ASSAULT EVERY 30 SECONDS |

Crime statistics according to the 1990 FBI Uniform Crime Report

Rape is one of the crimes, women and men, fear the most. Women for the obvious reasons, but no man wants to see the women he knows suffer through this horrible ordeal. As a violent crime, the FBI Uniform Crime Report showed the 1990 forcible rape volume increased 9-percent nationwide. In cities collectively, the total was also up 9-percent. The rural counties recorded a 7 percent increase and suburban counties, a 10-percent rise. The trends ranged from a 4-percent increase in cities with populations of 1 million or more to a 14-percent increase in cities with under 10,000 inhabitants. Regardless of where you live, violent crime is increasing. This is why you must take action now to avoid becoming a victim.

PROPERTY CRIMES

As the following figures indicate, you have a greater probability of being victimized through property crime.

One property crime occurs approximately every three seconds. Of these crimes, approximately one will be a burglary committed every 10 seconds, one larceny/theft every four seconds, and an amazing one motor vehicle theft every 22 seconds.

According to the 1990 Uniform Crime Report compiled by the FBI, there are approximately 485,566 full-time police officers in the United States. This means there are 2.2 officers on-duty who are statistically responsible for approximately each 1,000 people.

During 1990, the average value of property stolen due to larceny-theft was $480, up from $462 in 1989. When the average value was applied to the estimated number of larceny-theft, the loss to victims nationally was $3.8 billion for the year. This estimated dollar loss is considered conservative since many offenses in the larceny category, particularly if the value of the stolen goods is small, never comes to law enforcement's attention. Twenty four percent of the theft reported to law enforcement in 1990 ranged from $50 to $200, while 36 percent of the reported thefts were over $200.

Losses of goods and property reported stolen as a result of pocket-picking averaged $355; purse-snatching, $278; and shoplifting, $115. Thefts from buildings resulted in an average loss of $791; and from motor vehicles, $541. The average value loss due to thefts of motor vehicle accessories was $319 and for thefts of bicycles, $215.

The good news is you do not have to stand by and let yourself become a victim of crime. This book helps you to fight back. By providing many different and easy to utilize techniques, you **can AVOID** crime before it happens.

PROTECTION WHILE WALKING

Walking is necessary when going to and from your vehicle at work, shopping, school, or in your neighborhood. Walking can also be a vital part of an exercise program and an enjoyable pastime. However, this activity often makes you vulnerable to a potential attack. A small amount of preplanning will go a long way. Choose your route wisely, possibly carry personal protection spray to use against humans and animals (See Self-defense and Weapons), and always walk with someone else. Always look around and be aware of whom and what is in your environment. If a situation makes you feel uncomfortable, avoid it. Do not be afraid to run away and scream for help.

❑ Always walk with a companion. Most attackers do not want to confront two people, male or female. The buddy system is still the best.

❑ Walk within well lit areas and travel near curbs, and away from alleys, entryways of buildings, and bushes where an attacker could seek cover.

❑ Stay near people and avoid shortcuts through parks, vacant lots, and other deserted places. Criminals do not like to attract attention to their activities. Dark and deserted areas are good hiding places for bad people.

❑ Hold your purse or wallet close to your body — not dangling. This makes it more difficult to snatch.

❑ If your purse has a long strap, wear it across your body rather than hanging it over a shoulder. This creates a harder target to "snatch."

❑ Do not accept rides from strangers or hitchhike. If a driver asks you for directions, avoid getting too close to the car. You could be pulled inside the vehicle if you are too close to the car.

❏ While walking, if you are being followed, cross the street, change direction, or vary your pace. If the individual persists, go to a lighted store or home and call the police. If the situation demands, yell "FIRE" or "CALL THE POLICE." (Yelling fire will usually draw a considerable amount of attention.)

❏ If you are being followed by someone in a car, turn around and walk in the other direction or go up a one-way street. If the person continues, write down the license number and call the police immediately.

❏ One way to discourage a follower is to act suspicious of their presence. Keep turning around and looking behind you.

❏ When you return home, be sure to have your key in your hand and ready to open the door without delay. At night, outside lights should be left on so you can easily see anyone who might be waiting for you as you return.

❏ Be aware of your dress and actions in public situations. Showing large sums of money or wearing expensive jewelry can single you out as a target. Unfortunate as it may be, provocative attire may also yield unwanted attention. If you cannot avoid the aforementioned situations, make sure you have additional countermeasures in place. One way to counter this threat is to bring along another person capable of defending you and your possessions. You may also want to consider the ability to use self-defense techniques or weapons.

❏ Carry yourself in a confident and alert manner. When walking, stand tall and always survey your environment by looking around you. Make the effort to look people in the eyes, but do not glare at them. This enforces the realization that you know them or can identify them if required. Always be aware of the area and people surrounding you. Individuals who appear confident and assertive have a greater chance of discouraging attacks from criminals than those who look weak, scared and vulnerable.

❏ Plan your walking trips for daylight hours. It is recommended you carry a whistle with you. You should carry a detachable key chain with your keys on one side, and a whistle on the other. A set of keys in your hand with the keys poking out between your knuckles is a formidable weapon and easy to carry anywhere. You can also place the whistle in your mouth while walking or opening doors in unsecured areas. These two suggestions involve using daylight and noise, a situation most criminals seek to avoid.

❏ It is recommended that you have a key ring with two detachable sides. Your house key should never be placed on the same side as your car keys. This protects you against an unauthorized duplication of your house key when you are forced to leave your keys with a parking attendant. A whistle and small flashlight should be kept on your key ring. The drawing below, is an example of a secure key ring.

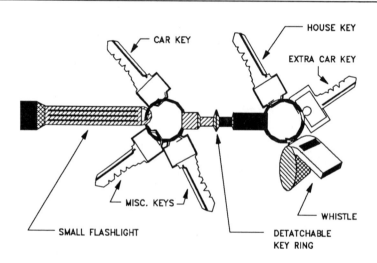

Security minded key ring

☐ If you find yourself in a situation where a weapon is needed immediately, you may have to improvise. A pen or the pointed end of a brush or comb may be used as a defensive weapon during an attack. You will achieve the greatest amount of force by using an overhand strike or downward motion. This motion is similar to throwing a baseball. It is important to remember that you will most likely have to repeat this strike several times to gain the desired effect. If you decide to fight back, all strikes should be delivered as quickly and forcibly as possible. The goal is to incapacitate the attacker which gives you the opportunity to escape.

☐ Elevators in apartment buildings, parking garages, and off hours in the work place, are other prime areas for attacks. It may be better to wait for an empty elevator rather than to ride with a stranger. If you must enter an occupied car, stay close to the control panel.

☐ Always have your keys in hand when entering or exiting your car. If you are parking in a public parking lot or a parking garage, always park in a well lit public area as close as possible to your destination. It is vital to always remember where your car is located.

CHECK LIST FOR WALKING

✔   Try to limit walking to daylight hours if possible.

✔   Walk in groups.

✔   Always have easy access to your keys especially when entering or exiting your car.

✔   Carry a whistle while you walk.

✔   If you must be outside after dark, carry a large flashlight. This may be used as an illumination device and a weapon.

✔   Always let someone know where you are going and when you will return.

✔   Plan a route which is as safe as possible.

✔   Use extra care in elevators, parking lots, and especially during off hours.

✔   Avoid high risk areas, if at all possible.

WHAT TO DO IF YOU OBSERVE A CRIME

This section focuses on situations you may encounter while a crime is being committed. Once again, you must decide for yourself what your course of action will be. If you are experiencing a crime, you must use your own best judgment in handling the situation. Our general suggestions covering most circumstances are as follows:

☐   Run away, whenever possible, toward people and lights. Criminals do not like noise, witnesses or lights.

☐   Do not attempt to resist if the attacker has a weapon. Resisting an attacker may excite or encourage the use of a weapon that was not originally intended to be used when the attack began. You do not want to turn a dangerous situation into a deadly one.

☐   Do not carry a weapon such as a gun or a knife for personal protection, unless you are trained and proficient in its use. Guns and knives can be lethal if used against you. You may want to purchase a chemical spray as these are nonlethal and normally have no long lasting side effects.

☐   If you are entering your residence and you suspect someone is inside, DO NOT go in! Immediately go to a neighbor's residence and call the police.

☐   It is unlikely that you will be confronted by a burglar in your home or apartment. However, if you are confronted, do not attempt to corner him. Many amateur burglars may flee if left an escape route. Try not to escalate the situation or provoke the burglar into attacking you. Avoid confrontation, at any cost! Try to escape at the first safe opportunity. There is nothing you own that is worth your life.

❑ If possible, discreetly observe the intruder and try to remember his/her description, including age, height, weight, color and length of hair, skin color, clothing, etc. This information will be vital if the police apprehend the perpetrator. Do this only if you can do so without further endangering your safety.

❑ When the intruder leaves, try to observe (without following closely) the make, model, and color of the vehicle. Also, watch which direction it travels. See if you can read and remember even part of the license number. Then immediately call the police. While waiting for the police, write down everything you can remember. It is important to do this quickly so that information is not lost.

❑ Unreported crime is a serious problem for several reasons. By not reporting a crime, you are assuring the ultimate success of the crime. Secondly, the criminal will most likely attempt to victimize someone else if they are not stopped.

❑ This same advice applies to any situation where you might witness suspicious activity and it is not reported. Always report any criminal activity. A clue you give the police, during your report, may lead to the swift apprehension of the individuals responsible.

WHAT TO DO IF YOU ARE ATTACKED

This is the most difficult and complex area to address. Because there are so many options and personal choices, the authors cannot suggest one course of action over another. This is strictly an area of personal choice on what your course of action would be if you are attacked. You have the option to decide whether or not to fight back. Whatever you decide, prepare yourself mentally to handle this type of situation and the consequences of your actions.

❑ Use your natural defenses and act fast!

❑ If possible, always try to run away. This should be your mind's first reaction. Run toward lights and people while you are screaming.

❑ Some people advocate fighting back when attacked. This may scare off an attacker or it may cause him to carry the assault further than originally intended. Each attack situation is different so it is difficult to suggest one course of action over another. If you do decide to fight, the following points may be useful:

❑ In a frontal assault, scratch with your fingernails or keys. Bite if your attacker's hand comes near your mouth. Scratching and biting will not only injure the attacker but will visually "mark" them for further identification when they are apprehended by the police. Kick with the point of your shoe into the groin or shin area. If you are carrying packages or other items, shove them into the attacker's arms. Swing your purse at the attacker's head toward his temple or ear areas.

❑ Another method of incapacitation is clapping your cupped hands forcefully over your attacker's ears.

❏ If you are grabbed from behind, jab your elbow backward into your attacker. Grind your knuckles into the attacker's hand if it is clamped over your mouth. Stamp your heel into the attacker's foot. Hopefully, the pain you generate will force the attacker to focus his attention elsewhere.

❏ If you have a weapon you are proficiently trained in, its use will depend on the type of weapon and the type of crime being committed. There is an old police saying, "It is better to be tried by twelve, than carried by six." This means it is better to go to trial for injuring or killing an attacker, than be carried by six pallbearers to the grave. As stated, each situation will be different and use of any weapon is a personal decision. (see Self-defense and Weapons, Page 21)

MAKE A SCENE!!!

❏ When you break away from an attacker, run toward people and lighted areas, continue to scream for help. People, lights and attention will discourage your attacker.

❏ If you are attacked in any way, immediately report the incident to the local police. Cooperate fully with the police investigation. Press charges when the attacker is caught. The conviction and subsequent incarceration of an attacker may prevent further attacks and may save a life.

WHAT TO DO IF YOU ARE SEXUALLY ASSAULTED

Sexual assault and rape are both mentally and physically cruel for any woman to endure. Oddly enough, rape is more often a crime of power than sexual gratification. Research has shown that only 20% of rapes are motivated by sexual desire. This fact is particularly dangerous when a rapist has a knife or gun. Unfortunately, you must be mentally prepared for the worst case scenario.

☐ Passive resistance may be advisable if your life is in clear danger. Vomiting, urinating, or telling the attacker you have a sexually transmitted disease or are currently menstruating may give you a chance to escape or stop him entirely.

☐ You may have decided to resist the rapist's attack. This can be to your advantage if a rapist expects a timid or passive reaction. Yelling, hitting, biting, poking the eyes, and kicking often gives a victim a chance to escape if done instantly. You must assess your situation quickly. Depending on the attacker's state of mind, your fighting back may increase the violence of the attack. This must be a personal decision based on the situation and facts present. You should be realistic about your ability to protect yourself. Never under estimate an attacker.

☐ After you have been assaulted, do not bathe, shower, or douche before reporting the crime. Do not dispose of any clothing or physical evidence; it will be needed for a conviction. Immediately contact the police and rape center after the attack. If you have a "Rape Hotline" in your area, use it.

Additional Information Sources

The books listed below explore a variety of options for trying to prevent and cope with sexual assault. Once again, the authors do not personally endorse these books and they should be treated only as guides since no one book or philosophy covers every situation. You are the best person to make the decision about how to deal with sexual assault for yourself. Your decision will be easier to make when you are better informed.

Title:	Surviving Sexual Assault
Editors:	Rochel Grossman with Joan Sutherland for The Los Angeles Commission on Assaults Against Women and The National Council of Jewish Women.
Publisher:	Congdon & Weed, Inc., New York, NY Copyright 1983

This book provides the addresses and phone numbers of Rape Crisis Centers throughout the United States and Canada. Since this book is over nine years old, this information may not be current.

To find the current information on Rape Crisis Centers in your area, call the local police department and the *National Coalition Against Sexual Abuse* in Washington, D.C. at (202) 483-7165. You can also contact the *National Organization for Victim Assistance* (NOVA) at (202) 232-6682 in Washington, D.C.

You can contact The *National Assault Prevention Center* (NAPC) at (614) 291-2540. The NAPC provides physical and sexual assault preventive training through the Assault Prevention Training Project (APT) for adults. A training program for children is available through the Child Assault Prevention Project (CAP) at NAPC. Ask for the program director and specify for which area you need information.

Other sources of information include:

Title:	The Voices of Rape
Author:	Janet Bode
Publisher:	F. Watts, New York, NY Copyright 1990
Title:	Everything You Need to Know About Date Rape
Author:	Frances Shuker-Haines
Publisher:	The Rosen Publishing Group, New York, NY Copyright 1990
Title:	Coping with Dating Violence
Author:	Nancy N. Rue
Publisher:	The Rosen Publishing Group, New York, NY Copyright 1989
Title:	Stopping Rape: Successful Survival Strategies
Authors:	Pauline B. Bart & Patricia H. O'Brien
Publisher:	Pergamon Press Inc., Elmsford, NY Copyright 1985

SELF-DEFENSE AND WEAPONS

Remember that using self-defense or martial arts training EFFECTIVELY requires extensive instruction and ongoing practice which may take many months or years. Even programs designed for women using basic techniques for fighting off an attacker cannot always be relied upon in all situations. If you do decide to fight back, make a strong commitment to learn and practice these defense techniques religiously. This includes practicing the mental awareness strongly stressed in this book.

☐ The decision to fight back is a decision based on your assessment of the situation. Putting up a fight could cause your attacker to injure you even more than he or she had originally intended; or you may escape. You are the only one who can determine the correct decision to make.

☐ Weapons are not recommended unless you receive proper training and practice regularly. The major disadvantage of weapons is that they can be used against you. Many people do not know how to use them correctly, or lack the commitment to use them effectively when attacked.

☐ If you decide to carry a weapon, consider using a chemical spray made from Cayenne Pepper concentrate, which irritates the mucous membranes of humans and animals. "Stun-Um" and "Body Guard" are individual product names for this personal protection spray product. Chemical "Mace" sprays do not always affect intoxicated individuals or those under the influence of drugs. Several studies indicate cayenne pepper spray will disable a person for 15-20 minutes. This spray induces watering of the eyes, nose, mouth and causes shallow breathing. It can be used repeatedly to incapacitate an attacker. If you accidentally spray yourself during the attack, it is not permanently damaging to your eyes, nose, skin, or lungs like certain types of "mace-category" substances can be. It is also an effective repellant for animals, while most chemical maces are not.

❑ When spraying a chemical substance, direct the spray toward the attacker's face. Do not wait for the attacker to get too close. Most sprays have a range of 10-15 feet. Also, hold the can close to your body and pivot your body to direct the spray. Do not hold the can in the extended arm position. It is very easy to strike your arm, which will misdirect the spray or cause you to drop the can. It is best to keep your arms bent at the elbows and next to your body.

❑ **You must find out what state, county and city restrictions have been placed on chemical sprays and other weapons you may decide to carry. The authors strongly advise you not to violate any of these regulations or restrictions.**

❑ Weapons can be very effective if you always have them at your disposal. With regard to the personal protection spray, have the top cap in the unlocked position ready to use when you are walking to your car, house, etc. This requires some practice to prevent accidental discharge, but it becomes automatic after awhile. It does no good to have the device in the bottom of your purse or pocket.

❑ If you make it a habit to carry this spray in the ready position and you develop your mental awareness, very few criminals will surprise you. Hopefully, you will surprise a would-be criminal!

❑ The advantage of using personal protection spray over other weapons is that it is nonlethal and, in most areas, requires no license. Its compact size makes it easy to carry. The spray can be very effective with minimal training in its proper use.

❑ If you are flying on a commercial airline, place any chemical sprays in your suitcase. If you attempt to carry this product on an aircraft, it will be confiscated by the authorities.

CHECK LIST FOR SELF-DEFENSE AND WEAPONS

✔   Decide if you want to use martial arts and/or lethal weapons. Be consistent with your moral and mental attitudes and feelings about injuring others.

✔   Select a weapon you feel comfortable with physically using.

✔   Learn to use it properly.

✔   Train consistently.

✔   Whatever method you choose, become proficient in its use.

✔   If you decide to purchase a personal protection spray, practice carrying and using the spray effectively. This is necessary to prevent accidentally discharging it on yourself. Buy an extra can and practice with it. Once again, hold the can with both hands close to your body when discharging it. To aim, swivel your body, turning in the direction you want to spray. By holding the spray in this manner, you decrease the possibility that it will be taken from you and used against you.

Additional Information Sources

The books listed below explore a variety of options for self-defense. Once again, the authors do not personally endorse these books and they should be treated as guides since no one book or philosophy covers every situation. You are the best person to make the decision about how to deal with the use of self-defense techniques for yourself in a given situation.

Title:	Self-defense
Author:	Sue Peterson
Publisher:	Morton Publishing Company, Englewood, CO Copyright 1989

Title:	Self-defense — Steps to Success
Author:	Joan M. Nelson
Publisher:	Leisure Press, Champaign, IL Copyright 1991

Title:	Armed & Female
Author:	Paxton Quigley
Publisher:	E. P. Dutton, New York, NY Copyright 1989

SECURITY AWARENESS IN ENTERTAINMENT AREAS (RESTAURANTS, BARS, AND MALLS)

Dining and shopping experiences are some of our favorite social activities. It is the pleasure that surrounds these events which can distract you from thinking about personal safety. Developing mental awareness into a habit will help keep these activities fun and safe.

❑ Park in well lit and secure areas. Do not leave any paper or information with your name or address inside of your car. It could be seen by a passerby. If a potential attacker observes your personal information, he then not only knows what car you drive, but where you live.

❑ Avoid shopping alone, especially after dark. Once again, criminals prefer to attack solitary victims in dark areas.

❑ Only carry the minimum amount of cash, personal information, and keys with you. If these items are lost or stolen, you will reduce your losses and chances for someone to find out where you live. Try to use checks and credit cards for all purchases and carry small amounts of cash.

❑ Pay attention to your credit cards and your receipts. Check the voucher before you sign it and make sure the clerk returns your card to you. Always request the return of the receipt and carbon copy. Do not entrust their destruction to the sales clerk. Some unscrupulous sales person may make charges on your account using credit card numbers they have "scammed" from legitimate transactions.

❑ When using bank cards at the Automated Teller Machine (ATM), block others from viewing the screen and keypad when entering your Personal Identification Number (PIN). Do not use an easy to ascertain PIN such as "1234." If there are individuals around the ATM machine that make you feel uncomfortable, wait until they leave or find another machine. Also, have different PIN for each card.

☐ Do not use your birth date or part of your social security number as your PIN. If your wallet is stolen these numbers are usually reflected on your driver's license or other cards.

☐ Do not put your purse or wallet down anywhere, especially in a shopping cart or on a restroom floor. For example, if you are in a stall, someone could reach underneath and snatch your purse before you have time to see who did it.

☐ Items which are bulky or cumbersome should be delivered to your home. If you carry these items by yourself, your hands will be full and you will not be able to get away easily.

☐ Purchase expensive items last. Whenever possible, place all packages in your trunk and lock your doors at all times. This reduces the exposure of these items, and yourself, to potential theft.

☐ Protect your valuables when trying on clothes. Do not leave them in the dressing area to find more clothes or to find a mirror. Take them with you.

☐ Do not leave unattended money on tables in restaurants. Give all money directly to your server, including their tip. Cash laying around is too tempting and easy for someone to take.

CHECK LIST FOR PUBLIC AREAS

✔   Park in well lit areas. Avoid shopping alone at night.

✔   Carry only what you truly need such as driver's license and credit cards.

✔   Check all credit card vouchers before you sign them.

✔   Be careful around ATM machines. Do not let anyone see your PIN.

✔   Do not leave your purse or wallet lying around anywhere.

✔   Have bulky items delivered to your home.

✔   Purchase the most expensive items last.

✔   Protect your valuables when trying on clothes.

✔   Do not leave unattended money on restaurant tables.

PURSE SNATCHING

The best way to avoid having your purse stolen is by not carrying one if at all possible. There are many situations where it may be desirable not to carry your purse due to security reasons. Here are some ideas to increase your personal safety and crime avoidance posture:

☐ It is advisable to carry your house and car keys separate from other articles. These should be carried in your hand, or in a pocket, separate from your purse. If your purse or wallet is lost or stolen, you will have possession of your keys. Since your address can readily be found in most purses, this is sound security advice. When walking or jogging, you can carry your house key on a chain around your neck, interlocked in your shoelaces, in a pocket, or just in your hand.

☐ Next, put a small amount of cash and a credit card in a wallet or compact cosmetic case. Then, carry either one in a concealed coat pocket. Some women have small hidden pockets sewn on the inside their coats for this very purpose. If you can get by without a wallet or compact, you can carry a small amount of cash, check book, or credit card. Place them in the pocket of your jacket or sweater. This is the safest method by far.

☐ Never set your purse or wallet on store counters, restaurant tables, or bus seats. When at clubs, never leave your purse, wallet, or money on the table unwatched if strangers are close by. Your address is accessible through information found in your wallet. An individual may not steal your wallet, but they may "look" you up later.

❑ If you must carry a purse, do not dangle it by your side so a thief can run by and grab it. Carry the purse close to your body, preferably in front. Do not wrap the strap around your wrist; you are likely to get hurt if a thief yanks hard. Bulky purses are the easiest to spot and grab. Shoulder bags are harder to get free.

❑ If someone grabs at your purse, do not attempt to resist or fight them off. If you carry a whistle, blow it repeatedly and observe the thief as closely as possible. After the assailant has left, try to remember a description for the police. Think of age, height, color and length of hair, skin color, build, and clothing. If you can note these things, you will greatly aid in the possible apprehension of the thief.

CHECK LIST FOR PURSE SNATCHING

✔ Limit the valuable items you carry in a purse or wallet.

✔ Carry only items you truly need such as limited cash, credit cards, and driver's license.

✔ When you carry a purse, keep it close to your body. Do not let it dangle by your side.

✔ If someone snatches your purse, do not resist as you may increase the ferocity of the attack.

✔ A small "clutch" purse is less likely to be snatched than a dangling strap purse. The exception to this rule is if you set your "clutch" down.

DOMESTIC AND INVITED STRANGERS

Generally, housekeepers and baby sitters comprise the majority of domestic employees. Although this group is not generally characterized as criminals, you must be careful when someone is in your home and with your children. Since these individuals are usually unsupervised, you need to take additional steps to protect your children and your property.

☐ Be aware that domestic employees can pass along valuable information to criminals since these employees have access to information within your home. It is wise to tell them as little as possible of your routine. Try to have an adult family member present when they are performing their duties, if possible.

☐ It is essential to do a thorough background investigation on all domestic employees and baby sitters **before** they are considered for employment. This also applies to an agency which may employ these individuals. A background investigation includes verifying previous employment, social security number, current residence, and carefully checking references. A criminal record check can usually be performed by the state police and the county records office. If applicable, also investigate the company for whom these people work. A call to the Better Business Bureau takes little time and can be very helpful.

☐ You may want to have domestics or any other employee fidelity bonded.

☐ Ask your baby sitters if they have experience in child care, first aid, and educational training.

☐ Try to find a baby sitter that is recommended by a trusted friend or is a member of a trusted friend's family. This will increase your chances of finding someone trustworthy and reliable.

☐ Do not allow baby sitters to have visitors in your home.

☐ Ask a neighbor to note the activity at your home when the baby sitter is working. They may discover any unusual activities taking place while you are away.

☐ Give the baby sitter detailed instructions of what to do in an emergency. Also, list all appropriate emergency phone numbers including; police, fire, your family doctor, the national poison center, and where you can be located.

☐ Conduct an inventory of valuable items and find safe storage areas for these objects. If a domestic employee steals these items, you will know exactly what is missing. Change your locks immediately after a domestic employee is no longer working for you.

☐ Never divulge personal information, or your routines, to service and route personnel. They may use this knowledge to burglarize your home when they know you are gone.

☐ When dealing with service organizations and contractors for work in your home, make sure they have a good and established reputation. If you cannot directly oversee their activities, have another individual check on them.

☐ Make sure easily marketable items such as cash, jewelry, liquor, drugs, important documents, and firearms are removed or locked away if workers will be in your home.

☐ Consider using a security patrol service if work done on your house leaves it vulnerable to burglary or vandalism .

❏ Make sure work done to your home has not defeated any of your security and emergency procedures. Review all security-related items, conduct an inventory, and consider changing the locks.

❏ Before you let them in, make sure strangers have proper identification and have proof of their employment with the proper business. Criminals can be disguised as "legitimate" repair persons to catch you off guard. A uniform does not make a stranger legitimate. Do they have a reason for calling on you? Check with their represented employer before you let them in. The same checking-up policy applies with strangers who have phoned ahead. You should verify their credentials before they arrive.

❏ If you are home alone, you may want to yell "Don't bother honey, I'll get the door." Make them believe there is another person with you.

❏ Be careful of strangers posing as building or fire inspectors or door to door salespersons. Check and verify their validity before you let them in your home.

❏ Do not let anyone lure you out of your home.

❏ Do not answer the door if you feel uncomfortable with a particular situation.

CHECK LIST FOR DOMESTIC EMPLOYEES AND INVITED STRANGERS

✔ Domestic employees should not be privy to nonessential personal information. If possible, these employees should not be left unsupervised.

✔ Conduct a complete background check on all domestic employees.

✔ Consider using only fidelity bonded employees.

✔ Domestic employees should not be allowed to entertain visitors in your home.

✔ Have a trusted neighbor monitor the activity while a domestic employee is working in your home.

✔ Give domestic employees clear instruction on duties and procedures during emergencies. Remember to include phone numbers of where you can be reached.

✔ Conduct an inventory of all valuables before, during, and after you employ domestic personnel.

✔ Do not divulge personal information to delivery or route personnel.

✔ Always use reputable contractors when doing home improvements of any kind.

✔ Lock and secure all valuables while contracted workers are in your home.

✔ If home improvements leave your home vulnerable, set up additional countermeasures or hire a private security officer.

✔ Change locks when you change domestic employees.

TELEPHONE SECURITY AND PROCEDURES

Most of us do not think of our telephones as a security risk. However, they can be an effective tool for criminals to find out if you are at home. Both burglars and rapists use the phone to track their victims. It has become essential to use telephone security procedures in your home.

❑   Do not antagonize obscene or prank callers, simply hang up the phone. If the caller persists, notify the phone company and the police.

❑   If callers will not identify themselves, hang up. They have absolutely no right to invade your privacy without the courtesy of identifying themselves.

❑   Never give out personal information on the phone.

❑   Keep a police-type whistle near the phone and if you receive an obscene call, blow it as loudly as you can into the voice portion of the receiver. You can also tell the caller that the phone has a trap set up on it. In reality, this can be done by the phone company if a caller is extremely persistent.

❑   Single women should use initials instead of first names in telephone book listings or request an unlisted number.

❑   If you have an answering machine, never say your name on your outgoing message. Never give out your phone number or suggest that you are not at home. Do not leave specific information about your whereabouts or when you anticipate returning on your answering machine. Here is an example of a safe phone message: "Hi, we are unable to come to the phone right now, but if you leave name, number, and the time you called, we will call you back as soon as possible. Thank you." By inferring "we" instead of "I," a single woman does not appear to be living alone. You may even want a male friend to make the recording to add an even greater deterrence factor.

☐ Be aware that devices are becoming available which can identify the caller's number before you pick up your receiver. Check with your phone company to see if they carry the Caller I.D. service in your area. Depending on the brand and features you choose, these machines will cost between $70—$130. Caller identification machines are invaluable in locating the telephone number of an obscene caller.

☐ If you go on an extended trip or vacation, do not cancel telephone service to your home. By canceling your service, you may indicate to a veteran burglar that you are away from home.

☐ Be sure that all emergency numbers are listed next to each phone in the house. This information should also include your address so that anyone in need has immediate access to it.

☐ Never give out information over the telephone about yourself, your associates, your friends, or your neighbors. Check the credentials of all individuals before you divulge any information. Ask them why they need this particular information. Burglars can use this information to find where you and your friends live and when someone is not at home.

☐ Be aware that excessive wrong numbers or hang ups may be someone trying to establish when you are home is unoccupied.

CHECK LIST FOR TELEPHONE SECURITY

✔ If you receive a prank call, simply hang up.

✔ If a caller persists, call the police and the telephone company.

✔ If you have an answering machine, do not divulge any personal information, or that you are out, on the outgoing message.

✔ Have a list of emergency numbers, your address, and your phone number next to each telephone.

✔ Never give out any personal information over the phone to strangers, especially credit card numbers.

✔ Monitor the frequency of hang ups or wrong numbers. This may be someone "casing" your home by telephone.

✔ If you are single, use initials instead of first name in all telephone listings.

✔ Keep a police whistle by the phone to treat those belligerent callers to a "piercing" surprise.

TRAVEL

Traveling alone and in unfamiliar areas creates its own hazards. This is when preplanning can be a real lifesaver. Take an extra dose of mental awareness when you are traveling.

☐ Avoid budget hotels. Criminals, drug dealers, and intoxicated individuals gravitate toward these low price accommodations.

☐ Survey the hotel thoroughly before purchasing a room. Check the parking lot for loiterers and extensive foot traffic. If there are individuals in the area that make you feel uncomfortable, relocate to another hotel. Ask the front desk if they have on-site security officers. Make sure all areas are well lit. A hotel that is remiss in replacing broken or burned out lights may not be security conscious.

AVOID HOTELS WITH THESE CHARACTERISTICS:

1. An unusual amount of foot traffic through the parking lot. This could represent drug or gang activity.

2. Convenience and liquor stores in the vicinity. These areas may draw loiterers and vagrants.

3. Hotels without a resident security staff.

4. Hotels that only have outside room entrances. This makes it easy for an attacker to wait undetected in a car until you get close to your door before they confront you.

STAY AT HOTELS WITH THE FOLLOWING FACTORS:

1. A resident or active security staff. Most criminals prefer an environment where they are least likely to be noticed.

2. A well lit parking lot.

3. Inside corridors for room entrance. Access to these areas should be limited by the hotel's staff and structural design. Normally criminals will not enter a well lit interior hall-way when there are other more opportunistic areas.

4. Visible patron and employee activity (i.e. bellhops, maintenance, security, room service, housekeeping staff, etc.). These people are likely to be around and make criminals think twice about committing any crime.

Some helpful suggestions:

1. When talking with front desk personnel, ask if you can rent a room close to the front desk or similar active area. Once again, activity discourages criminals.

2. Try not to book rooms on the first floor of a hotel.

3. If you are going to be away from the hotel, fill out the following list, enclose it in an envelope, and give it to the front desk. Mark instructions to front desk personnel to open it if you do not return by the time indicated on the outside of the envelope. This practice may aid the police in locating you if you are in trouble.

Your Contact's Information
Destination:
Address:
Phone Number:
Contact Person:
Estimated Time The Police Arrived:
Estimated Time The Police Departed:
Your Personal Information
Your Name:
Business Address:
Phone Number:
Driver's License Number:
Height:
Weight:
Hair Color:
Eye Color:
Ethnic Background:

Distinguishing Marks or Features:

Clothing Last Worn:

Your Vehicle's Description

Color:

Make:

Model:

Year:

V.I.N. Number:

License Number & State:

Distinguishing Characteristics (i.e. dents, special paint, custom features):

VACATIONS AND BUSINESS TRIPS

Vacations are intended to be fun, relaxing, and adventuresome. However, you must be aware of security and safety whether you are traveling domestically or abroad.

Prior to arrival, you should keep current on the news events of the area you will be visiting. If some type of civil unrest or governmental instability exists, do not plan to visit that location. Remember, the only place you have the full rights of an U.S. citizen is in the United States.

☐ To determine the current status of foreign countries to which you will be traveling, contact the U.S. consulate located in these areas or the State Department. Your travel agent should also know the status of your destination. Do not plan a trip without this information.

☐ When you are in a foreign country, do not advertise the fact you are an U.S. citizen by mannerisms, clothing, or attitude. Criminals, or terrorists, can easily spot tourists who exhibit specific habits.

☐ Be culturally sensitive and obey local customs and laws. Always be polite and respectful. This alone will save you many unnecessary hassles.

☐ Do not show above average affluency by wearing expensive jewelry and clothing. Dress to fit your surroundings. Criminals are the first to notice opulence and the opportunity for gain.

☐ Learn some basic phrases in the native language to help you find locations, order and buy foods or services, and to summon emergency assistance.

☐ Travel as lightly as possible. You can always purchase items as needed when you arrive.

☐ Use travelers checks as much as possible to reduce monetary exposure.

❑   Use hotel safes to store valuables whenever you feel that they are reliable. In some countries you may want to avoid using safes or the front desk to store your valuables.

❑   When traveling by car, if you stop, lock all valuable items in the trunk. When it comes to criminals, out of sight is out of mind.

❑   Always empty the car when you stop for lodging. If a thief does not see anything to take, he will generally leave your car alone.

❑   When renting a car, select one which is common and will not attract attention.

❑   It is prudent to use tour buses and taxis when traveling in unfamiliar areas. Make sure these are recommended by the facility with which you are staying or other people who have visited the area. Use officially licensed transportation services whenever possible.

❑   Only take the credit cards and identification you will absolutely need for the trip. This will reduce your losses if they are stolen. Do not leave credit cards in a hotel room. Put them in a safe. Many people make photocopies of all personal information they take on a vacation. If their wallet or purse is stolen, they automatically have duplicates of all important information.

❑   If possible, identify luggage with your business, not your home, address and phone number. If someone finds your business address on your luggage, they can only locate your business, not your home.

❑   If you are going to be away for any length of time, leave your car at home rather than at a parking garage. Take a taxi or have a friend transport you to your debarkation point and pick you up when you return.

☐   Make sure a family member or friend has your travel itinerary and phone numbers where you can be reached. If emergency arises, you need to be contacted. This will also help authorities to track you should you encounter difficulties.

CHECK LIST FOR VACATIONS

✔ Be aware of your safety and security while on vacation. You are more vulnerable while away from home.

✔ Before you travel abroad, check with the U.S. State Department. They will identify any trouble and unrest in the countries to which you will be traveling.

✔ When you are in other countries, do not flaunt your U.S. citizenship.

✔ Always be polite and culturally sensitive when traveling.

✔ Dress modestly. Do not flaunt wealth.

✔ Learn basic phrases in the native language to function in the society.

✔ Travel as lightly as possible.

✔ Use hotel safes for storing valuables when possible and reliable.

✔ If you take your car on vacation with you, make sure you lock your vehicle at all times. This applies to rentals too.

✔ Hide all items from view when stopped for any length of time. Lock valuables in the trunk.

✔ Select a vehicle of common appearance. It is a good security practice not to drive a vehicle that is overly "flashy" in certain areas.

✔ Use only reliable and/or recommended taxi or bus services.

✔ Be very careful when carrying and using credit cards and identification.

✔ Use travelers checks whenever possible.

✔ Use only a business address on luggage identification tags.

✔ Do not leave your car parked at the airport or pier. Have a friend drop you off.

DOGS AS A DETERRENT

Dogs are primarily an alarm and deterrence factor. A dog's natural instinct is to protect its territory. However, some breeds are better for this than others. Contact the local American Kennel Club chapter to find the breed of dog best suited for your lifestyle. Rottweilers, Doberman Pincers, and German Shepherds have a bad reputation as chronically mean and vicious animals. Usually, an animal's disposition is shaped by the owner. If the animal is abused by the owner, or overly aggressive behavior is tolerated, the animal is more likely to be vicious.

❑ A barking dog can be a very effective deterrent. This may be a welcome new security measure for people who do not currently have a dog.

❑ Dogs are most effective because they provide a warning if an unknown individual enters your property. For most people, this will be the dog's greatest contribution to home security. Many criminals avoid animal protected-residences.

❑ Most dogs are naturally protective of their owner and their owner's property. Some dogs will merely bark while others will bite strangers. While no one wants a wildly vicious animal, be tolerant of some barking especially when the dog sees a stranger. Too much scolding could diminish the dog's protective nature. Treat your dog with kindness and respect. They are more likely to defend you if there is a trusting relationship involved.

❑ A trained attack dog is not recommended as a pet for most people. They are expensive, potentially dangerous to invited visitors, and require a great deal of maintenance training to be effective. You should give a great deal of thought to these factors before you buy one.

❑ The owner, or handler, must understand their animal's actions and react accordingly .

☐ A poorly trained dog can be more vicious and dangerous than an untrained animal.

☐ If you decide to purchase a security dog, make sure the kennel has experience and a proven track record for the training and placement of such animals.

☐ Be committed and prepared to care for the animal properly.

☐ Professional trained watchdogs must be retrained periodically and exercised often.

☐ If you find yourself being threatened by a dog, remember, Cayenne Pepper spray is effective against dogs, while normal chemical mace may not be .

CHECK LIST FOR DOGS

✔   Determine if a dog is feasible for your living situation.

✔   Select a breed which fits your lifestyle.

✔   Contact the local chapter of the American Kennel Club (AKC) for a reputable breeder.

✔   Do not stifle your dog's natural instinct to protect.

✔   Treat your dog with kindness. You can easily bolster the dog's protective nature by fostering a mutually respectful friendship.

✔   If you choose to have a professionally trained watchdog, ensure that it is well exercised and retrained when needed.

✔   Professionally trained watchdogs may have to be segregated from visiting guests.

CAMPUS SECURITY

For many women, attending college is one way to establish or advance her career. With all the activities associated within the collegiate environment, crime awareness generally takes a back seat to other mental activities. Colleges not only provide educational opportunities but, unfortunately, criminal ones also. It may be difficult to maintain a mental awareness regarding crime in the collegiate atmosphere, but it will pay off.

☐ Keep your door locked at all times, leaving it open for even a minute is an invitation for robbery or attack. Always lock your dorm room or office if you are alone especially after hours or at night.

☐ If you take even a short nap, first make sure the door is locked. Always find out WHO is knocking before you open the door. Never leave doors propped open or unlocked for friends who will be coming over later. This may let the wrong person enter.

☐ Do not lend your keys out, they may be duplicated without your knowledge or lost. Do not leave them lying around your dorm room or apartment. This also applies to dormitory building keys.

☐ Never let anyone else use a key with which you have been entrusted. If your key has been lost or stolen, report it to the police and have your lock replaced immediately.

☐ Have your keys ready before you get to the door, this holds true especially at night. If you are fumbling for a key, you are not looking out for your safety.

☐ Familiarize yourself with the campus during daylight hours.

☐ Travel in groups after nightfall. Establish the "buddy" system to get around campus. This is very important to individuals new to the campus. There is definitely increased safety in numbers.

☐ Do not journey to out of the way areas of the campus to meet with new acquaintances. Arrange to meet in public areas during the day. If you find you must walk home at night, use a safety escort service or ride program if offered by your campus. If not, call a friend to pick you up.

☐ If activities require you to be away from your residence, try to schedule them during daylight hours or arrange for an escort back to your residence.

☐ Do not give out any personal information while you are socializing. This could result in unwanted visitors. If you are interested in future contact with new acquaintances, ask for a phone number from them.

☐ Please be aware of the unfortunate possibility of "Date Rape." This is especially prevalent in the collegiate environment.

☐ Find out as much as possible about new acquaintances prior to going out with them. Always know their full name, address, and phone number. Leave this information with a trusted individual, such as a roommate. Let your roommate or other trusted friend know where you are going and when you will be returning. Always call if you are going to be late. Have your roommate or a friend meet your date so she can recognize him if necessary. If you live alone, introduce your date to a neighbor.

PROTECTING YOUR PERSONAL PROPERTY AT SCHOOL

☐   Identify all items of value with your driver's license number preceded by your state abbreviation. (See Operation I.D.)

☐   Require authorization and identification from service personnel before letting them into your room or office to service or remove items for repair.

☐   Make a list of all your personal property by serial number and description, send an extra copy home, and register it with the campus security office. This list should include the item, brand name, model number, serial number, and a description.

☐   Mark all of your belongings with your driver's license number. If these items are ever stolen or lost, they can be identified and returned to you if they are found. If your state uses your social security number as a driver's license number, request a different number to be used on your license. It is easy for someone to locate you by using your social security number. Use the new number to mark your belongings.

☐   It is best to keep as few valuables around as possible. Check your family's insurance policy to see if your valuables are protected while you are away at school. Check with your school's insurance manager to find out if property protection policies are available through the school.

☐   School property deserves your protection, too. Be alert when using school equipment. Help protect it from theft, unauthorized use, or vandalism. Report any suspicious activities to campus police such as an unfamiliar person hanging around your dormitory, classroom, or other campus building. In the long run, you and other students help pay for school property, so it makes sense to help protect it.

CHECK LIST FOR CAMPUS SECURITY

✔   Keep your door locked at ALL times.

✔   Know who is at your door before you open it.

✔   Keep your keys safe by not lending them to anyone.

✔   Always have keys out and ready to open the door before you reach it.

✔   Mark all of your belongings.

✔   Never travel alone if possible. There is safety in numbers, especially at night.

✔   Plan activities, which are some distance from your residence, for daylight hours.

✔   Do not give out personal information.

✔   Be careful when walking with new acquaintances.

✔   Find out information about new acquaintances before you go out with them.

✔   Let someone know where you are going, with whom, and when you will return.

✔   Be aware of potential factors which contribute to many "Date Rape" situations. (over aggressiveness, considerable alcohol consumption).

CRIME PREVENTION FOR CHILDREN

Children, because of their size and trusting nature, are targets for the worst types of crimes such as molestation and sexual exploitation. Those criminals who victimize and abuse children should be prosecuted to the fullest extent of the law. Hopefully, the techniques listed below will help prevent your children from becoming victims.

Many police departments offer identification kits for children. These kits should include your child's most recent photograph, physical description, fingerprints, and address. Please remember to keep this information current, especially with small children, since they grow and change quickly.

☐ Never leave children alone, not at home, in a vehicle, at play, or anywhere else. Unattended children make an easy target.

☐ Make sure young children stay with you at all times. This is particularly true while you are shopping, at a movie, or other public events, and especially in the toy section of stores. Molesters and kidnappers can hide anywhere.

☐ Never allow children to enter a public restroom by themselves. This is a good place for kidnappers or molesters to hide.

☐ Reassure your child that if he or she becomes lost or kidnapped, that you will, no matter how long it takes, find them.

☐ Define who is a *STRANGER*. Let your kids know that just because they see someone everyday, such as the postal carrier, paper delivery person, neighbor, etc., it does not mean these people are not strangers. A stranger is someone that you or your child does not know well.

❑ Define who is a *FRIEND*. A friend should be explained to a child as someone who is known, liked, and invited into the home by the parents. Warn them about people selling door to door or delivering items to the house.

❑ If someone is trying to deliver something to the house, tell your children to ask the person to leave the package at the door. They should not open the door to talk with the STRANGER. One secure method of communicating with a stranger is to have your child talk from the safe side of a window. It should be secured open just enough to allow their voice to be heard. This keeps them out of that person's reach, while conveying the message that the family is security conscious.

❑ Teach your children their full name, your name, full address, and phone number, including the area codes. Teach them how to use a phone for long distance and 911/emergency calls. This information and training has saved many young and older lives.

❑ Tell them to call home if they have a change in plans or locations while they are away from home.

❑ Always make sure you know where your child is.

❑ Teach your children the "What If?" game, making up different dangerous situations they might encounter and helping them play out what they would do in that situation to reach safety. Make sure to include kidnaping in the "What If...?" game. This is where telephone knowledge pays off.

❑ If your child is kidnaped, the abductor will try to convince the child that you do not want them anymore. The criminal uses the fact you have not come back for them to psychologically manipulate the child. They may also tell the child you have given your permission for them to stay with abductor. You MUST teach your children if they are uncomfortable with a situation, or "staying somewhere" where you have not personally asked them to, then they should call 911.

❏ Take the time to talk to your children and be alert to any noticeable changes in their behavior or attitude toward an adult or teenager. It may be a sign of sexual abuse.

❏ Pay attention to, and be sensitive to, your child's fears or concerns, even if they do not sound real. Imagination can be used to cover up some very real problems.

❏ If an adult threatens them or asks them to keep a "special" secret, encourage them to tell you immediately. Reassure your child nothing bad is going to happen to them because they let you know. There are no secrets from Mom and Dad.

❏ Teach your children their body is private and **no one** has the right to touch them in a way that makes them feel uncomfortable. If anyone touches them in a wrong way, they should say: "NO!, GET AWAY!," then tell someone they know and trust. A good guideline to the private areas are the areas covered by a bathing suit. Nor should they touch another's "private areas."

❏ An extraordinary amount of attention paid to a child by an adult should be watched closely and carefully. Ask your child how they feel about this person in private. Ask if the two of them have any "special" secrets.

❏ Set up procedures with your child's school or daycare center about whom the child will be released to other than yourself. Setup a notification procedure they are to follow if the child does not arrive on time.

❏ Know who your child's friends are, their parent's names, phone numbers, and where they live.

❏ You should take the time to physically show your children the routes they are allowed to take coming and going to school and their friend's residences. Make sure they can find these routes when you are not there.

☐ Inform your children they must have your consent and approval before they enter another person's residence.

☐ Tell your children to ask other adults they go with not to leave them in a car or a residence alone.

☐ DO NOT leave your children in a car without adult supervision for any reason. Left alone, they are easy targets. Furthermore, police are normally required to protect your abandoned child until you adequately explain the circumstances. This may include an explanation in court for placing your child in a hazardous position.

☐ They should have a buddy system with their friends whenever they go anywhere. Tell them to always stay in the group. Predators gravitate to loners.

☐ Institute an escort plan with other trusted adults to ensure children have proper supervision.

☐ If you have small children leave the door to their room open when they are playing. This may alert you to any problems before it is too late.

STRANGER DANGER

The following recommendations deal with the most common situations involving abduction by strangers.

☐ If children are home alone, ask them not to tell this to any strangers who come to the door or call on the phone. Instruct them to tell the stranger that their parents are busy and cannot come to the door or answer the phone but they will take a message.

☐ Have your children call a designated neighbor or the police if a stranger will not leave when the child is home alone. Keep these numbers by each telephone.

☐ Tell them that adults should not be asking for directions from children. They should run away from this stranger.

☐ Establish a unique "code word" which only you and your child know. If another adult is picking up your child, instruct the child never to go with that person unless they use the code word. Remember to change the word once it has been used. Make sure your children never repeat this word, just ask for it.

☐ If they have a problem, teach your children the inside of their school is a safe haven. Your child should request help from a teacher if a stranger attempts to pick them up without using your common "code word."

☐ If you are going through a divorce, it is recommended that you change your "code word". Instruct your child your spouse does not have permission to pick them up without your "secret" word. Indicate to school authorities whether or not your spouse or prior spouse is authorized to pick your child up.

- [ ] Establish a safe house network in your neighborhood. Communicate frequently with neighbors to anticipate and avert crime-related problems. If your children are in trouble, teach them to use these neighborhood safe houses.

- [ ] If your child is being followed by a stranger, tell him/her not to hide in alleys or shrubs. Do tell them to run toward other people they know, or a safe house. Many communities designate a neighborhood "safe house." This is a home where children can enter if they feel threatened in any way.

- [ ] Teach your children to run in the opposite direction, if a stranger approaches them in a way that makes them uncomfortable.

- [ ] If they are in trouble, teach them how to yell for help as loudly and as clearly as they can. You may want to give your children whistles to blow if they feel threatened in any way.

- [ ] Children should leave as a group if they notice a strange adult is hanging around the school area or playground; especially if the adult wants to play with the children.

- [ ] Tell your children not to talk to, or take gifts from, a stranger. They should never go anywhere with someone who is defined as a stranger. Explain that no matter how pleasant or friendly this individual is, they are still not to be trusted.

- [ ] Children should never go near, or get into, a car with someone they do not know.

- [ ] A stranger can catch a child off guard if they use the child's name. You should **not** put your children's first or last names on articles of clothing, toys, or bicycles.

☐   Teach children to stay away from abandoned buildings, woods and dark places. There is usually more than "Stranger Danger" lurking in these areas.

☐   Allow your children to play only at city-approved and adult supervised play areas.

☐   Never leave home without telling your children where you will be.

A personal note: each of these suggestions takes time, patience, and effort on your part. Please realize these concepts are easily understood by adults but are sometimes confusing to children. You must take the time and teach your children EACH aforementioned recommendation. You can guarantee if something happens to your child, you will spend the rest of your life wishing you had made the effort. As a police officer, there is nothing worse than having to tell a parent their child is missing, or worse yet, dead.

Additional Information Source

The book listed below explores a variety of options for child care. Once again, the authors do not personally endorse this book since one book or philosophy can not cover every situation. You are the best person to make the decision about how to deal with your child's daycare provider(s).

Title: Choosing Child Care

Author: Dr. Stevanne Auerbach

Publisher: Barron's Publishing
        Copyright 1991

CHECK LIST FOR CHILDREN'S SAFETY

✔ Contact your local police department and request a child "Identification Kit." Update your children's photographs at least every six months. Always note their height, weight and date on each photo. (See Appendix 9).

✔ Whenever possible, make sure your children are never left alone.

✔ Make sure your children stay with you in public places such as malls, movies, public events, etc.

✔ Never let your children use public restrooms alone.

✔ Make sure your children understand if they are lost or kidnaped, you will search for them until they are found.

✔ Teach your children how and where to get help if they become lost or separated from you. Make a game of it. Have your child pick a spot where they will meet you if you become separated.

✔ Explain and define what a STRANGER is.

✔ Explain and define what a FRIEND is.

✔ Have specific ways for your child to deal with delivery personnel at home.

✔ Make sure children never tell strangers that they are home alone and what to do if the stranger does not leave.

✔ Teach your children their full name, address, and phone number.

✔ Teach your children to inform you where they are at all times. You should know who they are with (friends, other families, or acquaintances) at all times.

✔ Use the "What If" game to teach your children to understand how to handle dangerous situations.

✔ Use a code word system when other adults are picking up your children. This word should be something significant to the child but not something readily known to others, like a pet's name.

✔ Be aware of any changes in your child's behavior, especially toward a specific person.

✔ Make sure children understand that they MUST tell you about any "secrets" another adult asks them to keep.

✔ Teach your children their body is private. You can use the bathing suit region as a guideline for private areas.

✔ Teach your children it is wrong for an adult to ask them to touch another person's private areas.

✔ Watch out for an adult paying too much attention to your child.

✔ Have specific procedures with the school or daycare center for releasing your child to someone other than yourself.

✔ Establish a safe house system in your neighborhood or complex.

✔ Teach children which routes are to be used to travel to and from school. Explain that they are not to deviate for ANY reason. Once again, if they experience problems, emphasize that they should run home or to a safe house, using only populated routes.

✔ Make your children aware of "Stranger Danger" situations and what to do when approached.

✔ Use only the child's initials when marking clothes, play things and other items.

✔ Make sure adults watching your children never leave them unattended.

✔ Teach your children to use the buddy system with their friends.

✔ Teach your children to stay away from abandoned buildings, woods or lots.

✔ Institute an escort plan for ensuring children have the proper supervision.

✔ Teach small children to leave the door to their room open when playing. This will improve observation difficulties.

✔ Allow children to play exclusively at city-approved, adult supervised, play areas.

✔ Never leave home without telling your children where you are.

CHILDREN AND DRUGS

Drugs and children, and adults for that matter, just do not mix. Young, developing minds and bodies should not be exposed to these substances. It is no secret how addictive, destructive, and available "crack" cocaine is today. It is necessary to begin drug education for your children as early as possible. Drugs are no longer found just in high school and junior high. Elementary schools have become a new target for drug pushers. Parental involvement in this education process is critical.

☐ Have your children go through Drug Abuse Resistance Education (DARE) or "Just Say No" drug education programs. If children first learn that drugs are harmful and not "cool," they will be much less likely to try them. Constructive conversations about avoidance, if handled correctly, will not make your child more curious about drugs. However, it will promote why drugs are harmful and should be avoided. If you feel uncomfortable about talking to your child concerning drugs, your local Police department is a good resource for drug prevention information.

☐ Make sure children understand "medical drugs," are given by people who help us, such as doctors or parents. Reinforce the idea "Street drugs" are bad and make people physically and mentally sick.

☐ Tell them never to use any kind of drug without your approval and permission, even aspirin.

☐ Call street drugs by their commonly used names, for example; marijuana, pot, crack, ice and cocaine. Show your children pictures of these substances for better identification.

☐ Relate to them that these substances can poison and damage not only their bodies, but also their minds. Tell them these "street drugs" prevent them from thinking clearly, learning, and growing up strong.

☐ Buy "Mr. Yuk" stickers for all dangerous chemicals. Teach your children that these products are "bad" and should only be handled by adults.

❏   Cover dangerous chemical containers with "sandpaper" or something unpleasant to touch. If it is "nasty" to handle, a small child may decide it will not be fun to play with.

❏   Ask your children what they think about people who use "street drugs" and why they think people use them. Try to focus on why children use drugs. This will help you understand what your children know about drugs. Depending on their ages and what they know about the subject, you may want to tell them these children are copying adults. Another explanation is these children are trying to be "in" or "cool," or those who do not have friends to play with.

❏   Do not be surprised if your child has been exposed to drugs or has already tried them. Children are becoming aware of these things at increasingly younger ages. Be prepared for this in discussions with your children.

❏   Use the "What If?" game to teach your children to say "NO" to people with "street drugs." Imagine several different situations your children may find themselves faced with involving drugs or peer pressure to use drugs. If you have difficulty thinking of these type of situations, read your local paper. There are normally many articles about children and drugs. Explain to your children it is very important to tell you immediately if someone offers them drugs.

❏   Be prepared for accidental overdoses or ingestion of poisonous substances. Have this number on all your phones: National Poison Hotline **1-800-732-6985**. You should also find out the number for your local poison hot line and add it to your phone number list.

CHECK LIST FOR CHILDREN AND DRUGS

✔ At an early age, start your children on a drug education program.

✔ Make sure children understand the difference between medical and street drugs.

✔ Use the common street names for street drugs when identifying them to your children.

✔ Explain the hazards and bad side-effects as a consequence of using street drugs.

✔ Explain why some people use these "bad" drugs and the problems they have.

✔ Teach children to say "NO" to drugs by playing the "What If?" game.

✔ Tell your children never to use any drugs without your permission.

✔ Have a poison hot line number on all of your phone lists.

✔ Use "Mr. Yuk" stickers to identify poisonous substances. Like the label reads "keep these chemicals out of the reach of children."

AUTOMOBILE AND BUS SECURITY

Traveling in cars or buses is a daily reality for almost everyone. These vehicles can be the target of criminal activities. The techniques listed below may help you protect yourself while you are waiting for, or in, transit.

In addition to a home, a car is generally the single largest investment a person makes. As with any other asset, certain steps must be taken to protect it.

❑ If you own a car, keep it locked at all times. This means when it is parked and when you are driving. If at all possible, keep the windows up while driving. This will help prevent anyone from reaching into your vehicle or pulling you out of it. While stopped at intersections, keep the car in gear. If you are threatened, blow the horn and drive away as quickly and safely as possible. If you can make this a habit, you will reduce your risk of not only vehicle theft, but assault as well.

❑ Keep your purse and other valuables out of sight under the seat or in the glove compartment. Leaving tapes, CDs, shopping bags and packages in plain view is an invitation to break into your vehicle.

❑ Never leave keys to your home with car keys when your car is left in a parking lot or at a service station. These keys can be duplicated quickly and later used by criminals.

❑ Whether you drive or use public transportation, it is always safer to travel with at least one other person. If you use a bus regularly, use a schedule which minimizes the length of time you have to wait, perhaps alone, at a stop.

☐ When you are harassed by someone on foot, honk your horn in short blasts and drive off. If you are being followed by another car, honk your horn repeatedly. You need to find a police or fire station, drive-in restaurant, gas station, or some other well lit area where others can help you.

☐ Never go home when you are being followed. If you do, you will be giving your address to the person following you.

☐ Always park in well lit areas. When returning to your parked car, look under the car when appropriate, and have your keys ready to unlock the door without a lengthy pause. Look inside the car first to make sure someone is not hiding in the back seat. Make it a habit to keep valuables out of sight. Remove the temptation by placing such items in your trunk.

☐ If you have car trouble, turn on your emergency flashers, wait inside the car with the doors locked and the windows up. If people stop to help, do not get out. Rather, ask them to call the police. If they really want to help you, they will make the call. Similarly, if you see a car in trouble, do not stop to help. Go to the next available phone and notify the police. NEVER pick up hitchhikers.

☐ Do not leave a key hidden on your car. A good thief knows all the hiding places.

VEHICLE BURGLARY PREVENTION

Buy a quality vehicle burglar alarm such as the "Ungo" brand type. The "Ungo" costs around $350.00 installed. There are less expensive systems which you can install yourself. One of these brands is "Autocross" brand portable car alarm system which mounts to a flat surface by Velcro and plugs into the cigarette lighter. It costs around $65.00. The "Ungo" is one of the most popular systems for the money, but the "Autocross" system is a good alternative if you simply cannot afford the other system.

A more sophisticated burglar may have infrared scanners which can break the remote alarm coding fairly quickly? Do not consider these car alarm systems infallible. It is necessary to take as many additional steps as possible.

❑ Using a flashing diode, or other small indicator light, is an excellent way to broadcast to a criminal that your vehicle is protected. Even if you have a vehicle alarm, you usually sustain a costly window break before it is set off. A flashing diode may discourage a burglar from breaking into **your** vehicle because he will know your car has an alarm. A diode of this type is easy to install. Hide the battery pack under the dash and run the wires through the air condition vent or other area where the wires will not show. Spend the time to make it look professional.

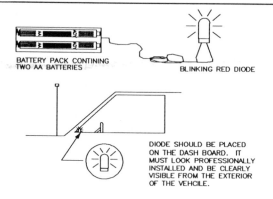

BATTERY PACK CONTINING
TWO AA BATTERIES

BLINKING RED DIODE

DIODE SHOULD BE PLACED ON THE DASH BOARD. IT MUST LOOK PROFESSIONALLY INSTALLED AND BE CLEARLY VISIBLE FROM THE EXTERIOR OF THE VEHCILE.

A simple, inexpensive way to make a car alarm indicator

☐ Use special locking lug bolts on all of your wheels. This prevents burglars from removing your wheels. Custom wheels are easy to sell for quick cash.

☐ Always keep your vehicle in good working order and filled with fuel. This will avoid breakdowns away from home.

☐ Make sure your vehicle has a locking fuel cap. Vandals often like to put sugar or other engine damaging substances in your fuel tank. This will also prevent the siphoning of your gas. Also, vehicles with locking hoods are more secure than those without.

☐ A steering wheel locking device, known by one brand name as "The Club," has proven to be very effective against professional and amateur car thieves. Many major metropolitan police departments have recommended using this device. They also recommend that you do not purchase an imitation as "The Club" is constructed with quality, heavy-duty materials.

☐ Unfortunately, if a professional car thief wants to break into, or steal your car, he or she will do so regardless of your precautions. Fortunately, very few car thieves are that determined and will pass up vehicles which are not the easiest of targets. Once again, keep all valuables out of plain sight and reach.

☐ Copy all of the vehicle identification information you get from the dealer and the manufacturer. Be sure to include your registration. It should then be placed in your safety deposit box or other suitable location with your important papers. Note your vehicle's Vehicle Identification Number (VIN), license plate number, and description. Keep all this information in your "records" area as well. (See Appendix 4)

❑ Slip several of your business cards into secret hiding spots, not in your visor or glove box, within your vehicle. Slip a business card or a piece of paper with your driver's license number and state between the weather striping and the window. Most car thieves will not look here unless they are completely stripping your car for parts. The automobile description record sheet, provided in the appendix, should show where you have placed these business cards. This will aid in identifying your vehicle if it is ever stolen.

❑ There are now "kits" on the market which allow you to mark your driver's license number permanently into the glass of your car. These kits come in two pieces, a stencil and a gel that scores your windows. It is an easy process and may make a car thief pass on your vehicle.

❑ Hard top cars are more secure than convertibles. It is very easy to cut or rip open a convertible roof.

CHECK LIST FOR AUTO AND BUS SECURITY

✔ Keep car windows rolled up, and doors locked at all times.

✔ Keep all valuables out of sight. This includes purses, tapes, CDs, presents, etc.

✔ Give the parking valet only the keys to the vehicle, not to your home. This also applies to repair shops.

✔ Keep your vehicle locked at all times.

✔ Whenever possible, park in well lit areas.

✔ Carry an emergency car kit.

✔ Never give rides to strangers.

✔ Purchase a vehicle alarm system and have it professionally installed.

✔ Remember, alarm systems only let you know that your car is being broken into; it does not stop anyone.

✔ Install a flashing diode.

✔ Use special anti-theft locking lug nuts on all of your wheels.

✔ Use a steering wheel locking device when your car is parked.

✔ Copy and keep your vehicle information and description in a safe or safety deposit box.

✔ Hide several business cards within your vehicle.

✔ Make certain your vehicle has locking trunk, hood and gas cap.

✔ Convertibles are less secure than hard tops.

PROPERTY MARKING

Property which is marked is extremely difficult to sell. Therefore, your property should be marked to reduce its appeal to criminals. In addition, this makes stolen property much easier for the police to track. This also increases your chances of recovery. Take the additional time and effort to provide this extra level of security for your valuables.

☐ If your property is stolen or lost, your engraved driver's license number, or state I.D. number, provides an instant identification of the rightful owner. This is true even if the property is recovered in another county or state, thanks to law enforcement computer networks.

☐ You should especially mark the types of items which are most commonly stolen such as TVs, stereos, VCRs, cameras, guns, etc.

☐ Create a list of all your valuable property. This should include all serial numbers and complete descriptions. A detailed list will aid in determining these items' property value in the event of theft. Also, be sure to include the model numbers. Keep this information in a safe place, such as a safety deposit box.

☐ Do not forget to mark items you keep in your car. This should include tape decks, cellular phones and CB radios. You may also want to place one of the smaller stickers in a visible area such as a wing window.

WOMEN AND CHILDREN FIRST:

"OPERATION IDENTIFICATION"

☐ Most police or sheriff's crime prevention units sponsor the "Operation Identification" program and will loan an electronic engraving tool at no charge. Some libraries will loan these engraving tools out to members. These can also be purchased for about $10.00 at many hardware and department stores.

☐ There is the strong possibility that you can prevent crime when a potential thief sees that your property is marked. Place an "Operation Identification" sticker, available at your local police department, on all outside doors and windows. A sticker shows all potential burglars your property is marked and you are security conscious.

☐ Mark your applicable state driver's license number followed by the state's two letter abbreviation. For example, a Washington state sample would look like this: SMITHJA123AB WA. As stated on page 52, if your State uses your social security number on your driver's license, there is usually a provision allowing them to assign an alternative number, however, individuals must request it. Ask your Driver's Licensing Bureau for a different number. It is easy to trace individuals by their social security numbers. This new identifier will make it harder for an unauthorized individual to locate you.

☐ Be sure to advertise the fact that you have joined "Operation Identification" by placing the stickers in prominent places. A good area to put them on or near all exterior doors and windows of your residence. Stickers are available from your law enforcement agency.

◻   Invisible ink markers are available from some law enforcement agencies and stores. They can be used to mark items which are not easily engraved, such as fur pieces, paintings, crystal, antiques, etc. It is a good idea to take color photographs, or make a videotape, of all items. This documentation process should include the four walls of each room of your home and all your possessions, such as clothes and storage closets. Photographs are also valuable in aiding recall of stolen, damaged property when making a claim to an insurance company.

Increasing a potential burglar's perception they will be caught could be the difference between burglarizing your home, or having them move on to another target.

RESIDENTIAL SECURITY

Whatever place you call "home," you obviously want to protect it. What makes a home a likely target? The fact is that no one can be there all of the time. People keep many valuables in their homes, and most houses or apartments are easy to break into. Do not give criminals "free admission" to your home. If someone really wants to break in, they will. However, you can make it as difficult as possible. These crime prevention steps will not only discourage many criminals, but may delay those breaking-in long enough for them to be detected, or better yet, get caught.

Most burglars are young. Almost all are under 25 years old (83%), and 51% are under 18 years old. Almost all are male (95%). The residential burglar is an opportunist. The burglar chooses targets which he or she can enter quickly, quietly, and not be seen.

Approximately 30% of burglaries are committed by drug addicts to support their habit. Due to their involvement with drugs, they are more apt to be unpredictable and violent. They are more likely to carry and use weapons, especially if they need money to get a "fix." The increasing use of drugs like heroin, "crack," and "ice," which are highly addictive, make confrontations with drug using individuals particularly dangerous.

☐ Make your home appear occupied at all times. Burglars do not like to be surprised while doing their work. The use of timers on devices to turn lights, radios, or televisions on and off in different rooms at different times can discourage all but the most determined criminal.

☐ Some burglars work solo, others in groups, so it is necessary to pay attention to both types.

☐ Most burglars will not pick locks. It takes too much time and increases the chances of being discovered. Therefore, lock your doors and windows at all times.

☐ Only about 10% — 20% of burglaries are done by pros. Pros make a real effort to "fit" into a neighborhood. If the neighborhood is upper-middle class, he may rent a BMW or Cadillac, wear a suit, and may pose as a real estate agent or insurance agent.

☐ A home which has unlocked fence gates and bicycles casually laying around sends a message to a burglar. It gives the impression you probably do not lock or secure your doors and windows either. To them, you have extended the welcome mat for crime.

☐ You may want to fortify a closet in the house as a safe room. It is preferable to use a walk-in type of bedroom closet. The door should be solid core with a dead bolt for protection purposes. For added safety, place a phone with a list of emergency numbers within this "safe area." This closet will provide a safe haven if an intruder enters your home.

☐ Your bedroom door should be lockable. You should also have a telephone in the room in case of an emergency.

☐ Many burglars say having neighbors who look around, and are aware of what is going on in their neighborhood, is a great deterrent. Be on the look out for strange vehicles or people. This alone may give a criminal reason enough to move on to another neighborhood. Get to know your neighbors by establishing a block watch program. Give your neighborhood a "bad" reputation among criminals.

☐ Have escape exits designated in your home for emergencies, or crime that forces you out of the house.

☐ Always change the locks when you move into a new residence. You never know who the prior resident gave a key.

The situations listed below often involve criminal activities. You may want to call the police if any of these situations occur and appear suspicious.

Be alert for or cautious of the following:

❑ Candy sellers, teenagers selling magazine subscriptions, salespersons, or any stranger may use these activities as an opportunity to case your home. An unanswered doorbell may be an invitation to enter an unsecured home.

❑ Persons who are selling merchandise at unbelievable prices.

❑ People loitering around a secluded area or in a parked vehicle.

❑ The sound of anything breaking such as glass or an explosion.

❑ A situation where people are fighting, display of any type of weapons, or an injured person. The people who harmed this individual may come back to finish the job and anyone else who may be helping him. Get help quickly.

❑ If you notice broken or open windows and doors on your home or a neighbor's home.

❑ If someone parks one vehicle, and then leaves in another one.

❑ If someone is "casing" parked vehicles, they may come back to burglarize them later.

❑ If you notice people removing anything from your neighbor's home while they are gone.

❑ Individuals taking short cuts across your property. They may have just burglarized a neighbor's home or are on their way to burglarize yours.

❏ Call the police immediately anytime you hear a scream in your neighborhood. Wait for the police to arrive and do not walk outside in these instances.

❏ Be cautious of persons unknown to you wanting to use your telephone or giving other excuses to attempt to enter your home. If you feel it is an emergency, have the person wait outside and call the authorities for them, DO NOT LET THEM IN!

❏ Do not allow insurance agents, home demonstration sales persons or any other unsolicited person into your home. If you are interested in their product, request they leave a business card in your mail box. This allows you to arrange for an appointment with their home office.

RESIDENTIAL SECURITY — OUTSIDE FACTORS

Remember that a home which is visible to neighbors and the street, will discourage the potential burglar. You should have at least standard lighting at your doorways and driveways. Depending on your home and yard, you may wish to add additional lighting in back or on the corners of your house. If possible, place lights high enough to prevent tampering.

❏ Unfortunately, heavy landscaping can provide a welcome hiding place for an intruder. You can control this factor by some additional pruning and, if necessary, transplanting.

❏ Do not leave extra house keys "hidden" nearby. Most hiding spots are relatively obvious and most burglars can easily discover them.

❏ Get a mailbox which is large enough to totally conceal mail, or install a small mail slot in your door which prevents access. Uncollected mail suggests no one is home.

❏ Do not leave ladders out that could be used to reach a high window. This is yet another reason to lock all windows.

CHECK LIST FOR RESIDENTIAL SECURITY

✔ Remember burglars are opportunists.

✔ Burglars come in all shapes, sizes, and styles.

✔ Make your residence look as occupied as possible.

✔ Keep gates locked. Bicycles and toys should be secured at all times.

✔ Make sure you and your neighbors look-out for your block.

✔ Be wary of door to door salespeople.

✔ Be aware of people loitering around vehicles or hidden areas.

✔ Be especially careful around violent situations.

✔ Question why strangers are at your neighbor's home while they are away.

✔ Watch for people using your property as a short cut.

✔ Immediately report broken or open windows and doors at your neighbor's home.

✔ Immediately report any screams, breaking glass, or explosions that you hear.

✔ Be aware of people casing any parked cars and report a detailed description immediately.

✔ Change your locks when moving into a new residence.

RESIDENTIAL SECURITY – DOORS

Lock Up! Amazingly, 30% to 50% of all home and apartment burglaries occur because someone did not lock a door or window. The following practical advice does not do any good if you do not make a habit of closing and locking windows and doors. This advice applies even if you are only going out for a few minutes.

☐ Many locks are incapable of preventing burglars from entering your home. The best door lock is an one-inch (minimum length) deadbolt which extends well into the door frame.

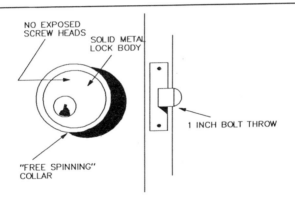

Diagram of a standard deadbolt

☐ The strike plate that the bolt goes into should be fastened with screws at least three inches long. Short screws will not hold up under the pressure of a crowbar or a well-placed kick. Each exterior door should have a deadbolt.

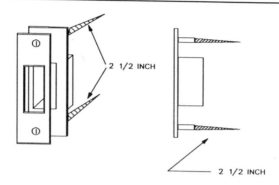

Diagram of proper door strike

☐ Check to ensure the lock assemblies on all exterior doors with door knobs have an anti-friction tongue as a standard. These are for door locks which are not deadbolts.

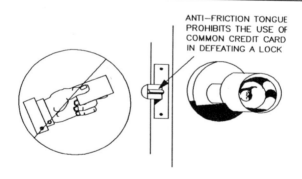

ANTI-FRICTION TONGUE PROHIBITS THE USE OF COMMON CREDIT CARD IN DEFEATING A LOCK

Diagram of an anti-friction tongue

WITHOUT AN ANTI–FRICTION TONGUE
DOOR IS EASILY OPENED WITH
A CREDIT CARD

Diagram of a door without anti-friction tongue

The best exterior door is metal or solid-core wood 1-3/4 inch thick. Fragile, hollow core doors should never be used as exterior doors. With one swift kick, flimsy doors and locks are easily broken.

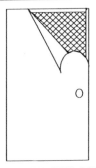

HOLLOW CORE DOOR

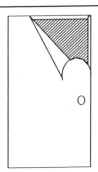

SOLID CORE DOOR

Diagram of hollow and solid door cores

❏ Doors should always be hung with the hinges on the inside of the structure. This prevents someone from removing the hinges from the outside and gaining access to your home. Another added security measure is to remove one of the screws holding the outside (door side) hinge and placing a nail in the corresponding jam side.

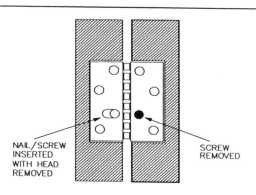

NAIL/SCREW INSERTED WITH HEAD REMOVED

SCREW REMOVED

Diagram of a security hinge setup

❏ Install 190 degree peephole in all exterior doors. You should also have adequate lighting around exterior entrances. This allows you to see who is outside your door before you let them in.

❏ A "flip lock" is an inexpensive way to partially secure your interior doors.

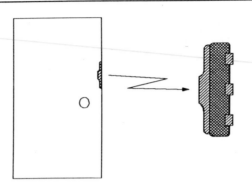

Inexpensive yet secure "flip lock"

☐ There are ways of strengthening less than adequate doors at modest expense. For example, add a 1/2 inch plywood plate over the wooden panels. If a door has a large piece of glass in it, you can install a metal grill or a security panel of 3/16 inch polycarbonate material.

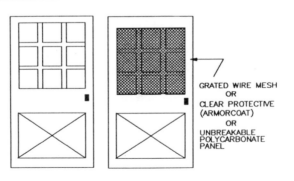

GRATED WIRE MESH
OR
CLEAR PROTECTIVE
(ARMORCOAT)
OR
UNBREAKABLE
POLYCARBONATE
PANEL

Diagram of protective door/window coverings

❏ Sliding glass doors present a special problem since they can be lifted out of the track. To prevent this from happening, a wood or metal bar of the proper thickness can be screwed inside the upper track at the top of the sliding door. This will let the door slide properly but will not allow the door to be lifted out of the track.

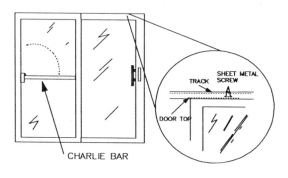

CHARLIE BAR

Example of Charlie Bar and non-lift screws on a sliding glass door

❏ The Charlie Bar is a metal bar which prevents the sliding door from being opened. It is very easy to use and relatively effective. The key is to use this device at all times. Do not use the Charlie Bar as the only means of security for sliding doors.

❏ A sliding glass door can also be secured by drilling holes for pins in the upper and lower tracks. This prevents the door from sliding when the pins are inserted.

CHECK LIST FOR RESIDENTIAL DOORS

✔ Always lock ALL of your doors, without exception.

✔ Make sure all exterior doors are locked with a one inch deadbolt.

✔ Make sure all exterior doors are metal or solid-core wood 1-3/4 inch thick. The screws on the strike plate should be at least 2 1/2 inches long.

✔ Door hinges should always be on the inside.

✔ Install a 190 degree peephole in all exterior doors and make sure these areas are well lit.

✔ Properly secure all sliding glass doors with locks, Charlie Bars, dowels, and inserted pins or screw type pressure devices. These prevent the doors from sliding in their tracks.

✔ Make sure the material around your doors and windows are structurally sound enough to secure locking devices too. If the framing structure is weak, the lock will not make a difference.

RESIDENTIAL SECURITY WINDOWS

Most windows come equipped with latches. Since many window latches do not provide ideal security, it is a good idea to supplement them. Special locks, such as barrel bolt locks, are now available to provide extra security for various types of windows. In case of emergencies, make sure everyone knows how to use the lock. If it is a key lock, place the key in an easily accessible location that everyone knows.

☐ In addition to locks, there are two other inexpensive techniques for securing windows. For windows that slide sideways, use the same method of placing a rod or dowel in the tracks as described for sliding doors. The second method used is to secure double-hung windows. You start by drilling a hole and placing a pin through each top corner of the inside sash. These holes should be three quarters of the way through the outside sash at a downward angle. Insert two 5/16 inch diameter eyebolts on each side of the window. The bolts should fit loosely enough in their holes so that they are easy to insert and remove. A separate set of holes can be drilled into the outside sash approximately three to four inches above the inside sash. This allows windows to be left open for ventilation. It also prevents the window from being opened further than the three or four inches necessary for ventilation.

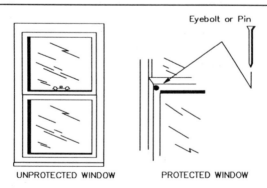

UNPROTECTED WINDOW   PROTECTED WINDOW

Diagram of inexpensive window protection

☐ Most locksmiths and hardware stores sell screw controlled antiburglary clamps. These devices are placed in the tracks of windows and sliding glass doors to prevent the door from sliding open.

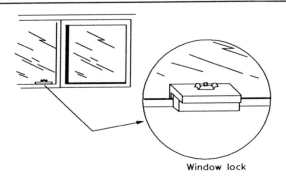

Window lock

Diagram of inexpensive window protection

☐ To prevent opening, many windows can use a Charlie Bar or, as stated on page 89, a piece of wood dowel or rod placed in the track .

CHECK LIST FOR WINDOWS

✔ Make sure your windows have additional protection such as barrel bolt locks.

✔ Secure all sliding windows by placing rods or dowels in the sliding tracks.

✔ Use special procedures for securing double-hung windows.

✔ When special equipment is used for securing windows, make sure these devices comply with fire codes and everyone knows how to use them properly.

✔ Make sure all windows, frames, and locks are in good working condition.

RESIDENTIAL SECURITY — GARAGES

Failure to close and lock garage doors presents a serious security problem. If an intruder gains entrance to the garage, they will be concealed and might find the tools necessary to continue the entry and burglary of your home. Due to the way garage doors are secured, the locks are normally easily overcome.

☐ An electric garage door opener is a good investment because you do not have to get out of your car to open the door. Buy a good quality garage door opener, one with changeable codes. Immediately change the factory settings to your own pattern. These are less likely to be opened by random signals.

☐ Make sure the door is completely closed before you unlock your car doors and get out. Also, your garage opener should have a light on it which is activated when the door is opened or closed. This light should automatically turn itself off.

☐ Whenever entering the garage, look around for possible entrance by a burglar or attacker. You can usually survey the garage from your door. A good tip is to install a 190 degree peephole in the door leading to your garage.

☐ Do not leave your garage door opener in plan sight when you are away from your vehicle. If your car is stolen, the thief can usually find your address on your vehicle registration. Then, they simply automatically open your garage door and burglarize your home, and you have given them the getaway car!

☐ The door leading from the garage to the house should be treated as an exterior door which is solid and has a one inch deadbolt lock.

☐ When you leave for extended periods of time, you should place a bicycle lock in the tracking of your garage door. This will prohibit the door from opening if someone has successfully forced open the garage door lock.

CHECK LIST FOR GARAGE SECURITY

✔ Always close and lock garage doors at all times.

✔ An automatic garage door opener can be a good personal safety device.

✔ Do not leave the garage door opener in plain sight inside your vehicle. If your vehicle is stolen, the thief now has your address, which can be found on your registration slip. They may also find a spare key to your home and your garage door opener.

✔ Treat doors leading from the house to the garage as you would an exterior door. Install one constructed of sturdy material.

✔ Install a 190 degree peephole in the door leading into your garage.

✔ When taking a trip, secure your garage by placing a common bicycle lock in the garage door track. This will prohibit opening the door from the outside.

RESIDENTIAL SECURITY — LIGHTING FOR YOUR HOME

Lights are a definite deterrent to criminals as it exposes their activities to observers. Install and maintain lights around all windows, doors, and any other darkened areas around your home and yard. Dark areas present perfect hiding places. The level of light should be sufficient to read a standard white business card with black print at arm's length. These "light zones" make your home more secure.

❏ Work with your neighbors to establish adequate lighting between homes. To keep energy costs down, consider using motion sensitive lights, which turn on only when there is movement near the light.

❏ Make sure the public utility which maintains and operates street lights is immediately informed of any burned out or damaged lights near your home.

❏ Be aware that trash dumpsters and recycling bins can provide cover for potential criminal activities. You should sufficiently light areas where these containers are located.

❏ All fence gates should be well lit.

❏ When you are inside your home at night, close your shades or drapes, and turn lights on and off as you move about. This will let criminals know that someone is home.

❏ Pick a different combination of lights to leave on all night. This prevents a predictable pattern from developing. This will discourage anyone who might be "casing" your home since they think you are at home.

❏ Utilize motion sensitive and timer controlled lights which ensure you do not have to come home to a dark house or apartment at night. You should incorporate this strategy even if you will only be gone a short time.

CHECK LIST FOR LIGHTING

✔ Provide a barrier of light all the way around your home.

✔ Work with your neighbors to establish adequate lighting between homes.

✔ Make sure all street lights are working properly.

✔ Beware of dark areas which can conceal criminals.

✔ Light all areas around alleys, trash bins, and storage sheds.

✔ Light around gates and exterior entrances.

✔ Close your drapes at night and turn lights on and off as you move from room to room.

✔ Use different combinations of lights left on at night.

✔ Use motion detecting and timer controlled lights, indoors and outdoors.

RESIDENTIAL SECURITY — ALARM SYSTEMS

Intrusion, or burglar alarm systems are a very effective deterrent against criminal activity. Current technology has created effective and inexpensive systems for businesses, houses, and apartments. Select an alarm system which also incorporates fire protection capabilities. The best smoke detector, and the most expensive, for residential structures is the ionization type device.

☐ When considering a security system, you should seek guidance from your police, fire, and insurance professionals about the best type of system for your needs. Some equipment may even reduce your insurance premiums.

☐ Check out the potential alarm companies' warranties, reputation with other customers and the Better Business Bureau. Avoid a "good deal" on a price offered by "fly by night" companies. The alarm industry has become very competitive so you can deal with solid, reputable organizations at a reasonable price. Do not succumb to scare or high pressure sales tactics to get you to buy more than you need. Examine and understand all charges for installation and the length of monitoring contracts. Ask for an itemized quotation for all work done.

☐ If you have high value or specialty items in your home, you should make sure the alarm system covers a specified area. It is a good idea to have additional sensors for areas such as a lockable closet or valuables' storage. Your increased coverage will help provide better protection. Do not disclose any information about these particularly valuable items or areas.

☐ There are several different types of motion detectors. Make sure the installations make allowances for indoor pets, ceiling fans, sunny windows, etc. Ask for a "pulse-count" or "Microwave/Passive Infrared" motion detector which reduces false alarms caused by environmental factors, such as sunlight and heaters.

❑ Alarms may be unmonitored and only sound locally from your home or the system can be monitored by an alarm company. Be aware that most alarm companies make their money by monitoring services, not on the equipment. However, a monitored alarm system will notify somebody at the company when there is an alarm at your home. Monitoring is a necessary factor in order for the alarm system to be effective. You should request an Underwriters Laboratories (UL) listed company to monitor your alarms. To be listed with UL, the company is required to meet certain equipment and personnel quality standards for providing 24-hour response to your alarm system. Be sure to find out this information before you sign a monitoring agreement. Not all 24-hour monitoring companies are UL-listed.

❑ Ask your alarm installer to provide you with "lawn" or external deterrent signs which are clearly visible from the street. These signs indicate your home has an alarm system.

❑ It is wise to have a monitored system because you and the police or fire department will be immediately notified if the system signals an alarm.

❑ For added safety, smoke alarms and, if appropriate, natural gas detection equipment should be added to your Security alarm systems.

❑ You may want to take advantage of a system that has a silent distress function. Normally this is seen in two forms. The first type is a push button actuation, similar to a car alarm activator, carried with the individual throughout the home. These are seen in many alarm advertisements for the elderly. The second type of distress actuator is usually built into the digital alarm panel controlling the alarm system. This is activated if you enter a duress code.

❑ If you choose an alarm system which is monitored by a security company, find out if they send out their own security officers to respond to an alarm. If not, do they just contact the local law enforcement agency?

CHECK LIST FOR ALARM SYSTEMS

✔ Seriously consider installing a monitored burglar alarm system.

✔ Shop around for a system. Talk to your local police, fire, and insurance professionals for their advice.

✔ Only deal with reputable alarm companies.

✔ Choose the equipment which will best fit needs and your lifestyle.

✔ Make sure your home also has smoke detectors.

✔ Use the yard signs and decals provided by the alarm company.

✔ Make sure your alarm system protects high value items in a special area by using additional sensors.

✔ If your home is heated by natural gas, you should have gas detection monitors added to your security system.

✔ You may want to purchase a system with a duress function.

RESIDENTIAL SECURITY — WHEN YOU ARE AWAY

It is extremely important to make your home or apartment look "lived in" while you are away, even if it is only for a matter of hours. The same precautions we take when going on a two-week vacation, for example, should be used for an overnight trip. It is a good idea to ask a trusted neighbor to maintain your day to day routine.

❑ Do not advertise that you are away by leaving a note on your door to relay a message. This says you are not at home and you are asking for trouble. If you must leave a message for someone, place it in your mail box or give it to a neighbor to hold.

❑ Use automatic timers or ask a trusted neighbor to turn your lights on at night and off in the morning and to turn on a radio as well. Ask your neighbor to vary the lights left on. For example, leave the bathroom light on one night and kitchen the next.

❑ Ask a neighbor to fill a garbage can and put it in front of your house on the usual collection day. However, do not let the can sit there for days.

❑ Ask a trusted neighbor to pick up your newspapers. Do not tell the newspaper carrier you will be gone. If you are going to be away for a long time, simply cancel your paper. Do not enter a "vacation stop" notice. If you notify them in advance, your local post office will hold your mail for you until you return.

❑ Ask your neighbor to park their car in front of your house from time to time to give the appearance that someone is coming and going regularly.

❑ Arrange to have your lawn watered, mowed, and raked if necessary. Your walkways and driveways should be shoveled during the snowy winter months.

❑   Do not allow any travel plans to be advertised in advance. This is especially likely to come up in connection with group tours. Do not talk about travel plans in public places either. You never know who is listening.

❑   Notify the local police department you are going on vacation. Many police departments have programs to place extra patrol emphasis on homes when the owners are on vacation.

MAKING A RESIDENCE APPEAR OCCUPIED

☐ Use automatic light and appliance controllers or timers. Some units are controlled by computer chips to vary a pattern of room lighting while also varying the light intensity. These models will help give the appearance that someone is home and cost between $12.00—$150.00 depending on their complexity.

☐ Some of these units have a remote control. They can also be used to light predetermined areas of your house before you get home as an added security and safety feature.

☐ Automatic appliance timers are not only used to turn lights on and off, but also televisions and radios.

☐ When you leave, have lights on and a television or radio playing to make burglars think you are home.

☐ Infrared motion detection and timer controlled lights simulate being turned on by the home owner. These devices also save electricity. Position these lights strategically inside and out.

☐ Closed drapes, shades, or blinds are sign no one is home. Leave some of them open while you are gone.

☐ Keep your garage doors, gates, and windows closed and locked. (See previous chapters)

CHECK LIST FOR WHEN YOU ARE AWAY

✔ Make your house look "lived-in" while you are away.

✔ Ask your neighbor to set your garbage cans out on trash day when you are gone.

✔ Have your neighbors park their cars in your driveway.

✔ Do not advertise that you are away from home by letting papers or mail accumulate.

✔ Keep your garage doors, gates and windows closed and locked at all times.

✔ Arrange to have your yard and property taken care of while you are away.

✔ Use motion detecting and timer controlled lights inside and out.

✔ Keep travel plans as private as possible.

RESIDENTIAL SECURITY — APARTMENTS

Get to know the residents in your building and explain to them how important communication is among those in your building and complex. Neighborhood watch techniques are very effective in an apartment setting.

☐ Be careful in laundry rooms, especially take note of people loitering. Do not leave your clothes unattended. If you can, do your laundry with a friend.

☐ Do not leave your door unlocked at anytime, day or night, whether you are there or not.

☐ Your balcony can be used as a way into the apartment, even if you are located well above ground level. Remember to lock all windows and doors on all building floors.

☐ Hallways, stairwells, and elevators are potential areas for criminals to loiter. Make caution a habit. Use common sense, the buddy system, and your "how to avoid crime" mental awareness.

☐ If you have an access control system using an intercom, do not let anyone into your building that you do not know or trust. Also, do not give strangers information about other residents or allow them in to locate other tenants.

☐ It may not be possible to implement some of these suggestions if you live in an apartment or retirement facility. However, you can talk to the manager about a specific plan to upgrade the security in your building. It will probably be more effective if you get several tenants together when you approach the manager. Official security standards have been adopted in some areas and should be of assistance to you. From a manager's point of view, this can also increase the value of the complex.

❏ Do not allow anyone to follow you into a building where there is a locked door for residents to use, even if they look like they belong there. If they do not have a key, they should not be walking in the building unaccompanied by a resident.

❏ If your apartment's security is not adequate, bring it to the manager's attention. Also, precisely document the existing conditions, manager's response, and actions taken to correct the problems. This will be an effective tool for filing a complaint or to use in a lawsuit if you become a victim of a crime which could have been prevented.

APARTMENT SECURITY SURVEY

The items listed below will help you to choose an apartment which has less exposure to crime. All of these factors should be considered when looking at an apartment complex.

?   Is there limited access from main roadways? There should be no more than one or two entrances.

?   Is there a washer and dryer located in your apartment? If not, make sure the laundry room available is well lit, has windows, key-accessible only. It should be free of shrubbery and high fencing.

?   Does the complex have a well lit parking lot? Better yet, does it have a controlled access parking area for residents with a separate lot for visitors? Covered parking and garages are also preferable features.

?   Do all exterior doors have deadbolt locks?

?   Do exterior doors have "peep holes" installed in them?

?   Are the locks changed with each new tenant, including mail box key?

?   Are there security personnel patrolling on-site?

?   Before moving in to a new apartment, have you asked prospective neighbors about the area's crime rate and what problems they have encountered?

?   Have you contacted the local police department to determine the level of crime which occurs in and around the apartment complex? This should be done before you decide to move in.

?   Do you have renter's insurance which covers theft, vandalism, and fire?

?   Is there a neighborhood watch program established in the complex?

?   Have you considered living on the second or third levels of the complex? (Due to ground level accessibility for undesirables)

?   Have you surveyed all stairways and hallways of your prospective building? It is safer to have stairways and hallways which are on the inside of the building rather than outside. There should also be controlled access to the inside areas of the complex and individual buildings.

?   Are the apartment numbers easily read so emergency personnel can respond quickly?

?   Are balconies detached from one another? Are you in the habit of locking balcony doors?

?   Have you explored the possibility of renting an apartment in a security complex? These buildings usually have electronic doors, patrolling security officers, and closed circuit television (CCTV) monitoring systems.

CHECK LIST FOR APARTMENTS

✔ Establish and maintain good communications with your neighbors.

✔ Try to do your laundry with a neighbor or friend.

✔ Never leave your front door unlocked.

✔ Your balcony door must be secured regardless of which floor you live on.

✔ Beware of hallways, stairwells, and elevators for attackers to hide in.

✔ Never circumvent your apartment building's security procedures for anyone.

✔ Do not give strangers access to your building no matter what they say.

✔ Always check with your apartment manager before implementing any of the changes mentioned. They may require a key before you add a deadbolt. Also, they may want their staff to do any work, such as installing a Charlie Bar.

✔ Use the "Apartment Security Survey" when looking at apartments. Do not believe what the apartment's staff tells you, find out for yourself.

OFFICE SECURITY

Unfortunately, all criminals are not strangers. The work place is no exception to personal or property crimes. Take the time to secure your personal belongings. You also need to utilize security around the office on your employer's behalf. By protecting your company's information and property, you also help protect your job.

☐ If you leave your work area for a brief time, secure all personal items and any company information. Do not leave company proprietary data located where unauthorized eyes have access to it.

☐ Make it a point to know and follow your company's security and safety procedures. Do not allow other employees to be careless with these policies and endanger you or the company.

☐ Be very discreet when discussing your job outside the work place.

☐ Make sure that any strangers in employee areas have proper identification and a reason for being there. It is best to have an employee escort all visitors, service or sales personnel.

☐ Retail employees should always obtain positive identification for checks and credit cards. Beware of and learn how to recognize counterfeit money. Contact the nearest FBI office for detailed information on counterfeiting.

☐ Greet all patrons or visitors who enter your area. Watch for bulky coats, large purses, shopping bags, folded newspapers, and partially opened umbrellas. These tactics also work for minimizing employee thefts.

❏ Have a lockable drawer in your desk or locker to protect your personal belongings.

❏ Understand your company's policies, procedures, and rights concerning employee theft, patron theft of employee items and shoplifting .

CHECK LIST FOR OFFICE SECURITY

✔ Make sure to lock away personal items at all times.

✔ Always protect company information and data from unauthorized personnel.

✔ All employees should follow security protocols without exception.

✔ Do not discuss company business outside of work.

✔ Use a system to limit and control the access of visitors and vendors while on company property.

✔ Utilize a positive identification procedure when doing check and credit card transactions.

✔ Be aware of shoplifters and how your company handles them.

✔ For retail businesses, greet and carefully observe all customers.

PROTECT YOUR MONEY

If it sounds too good to be true, then it probably is. You should never give money, especially cash, to a stranger. The criminals usually sell an unfamiliar product or service or represent a company unknown to you. It is prudent to only use credit cards or checks if you purchase anything from these individuals or companies. This may not even be a good idea since they will have your credit card's or bank account's number. If they refuse these, let them take their business elsewhere. You should also report any suspicious activity to the police immediately. Try to give the police a description of the person, their vehicle's license number, and what happened. There are plenty of legitimate businesses from which to purchase products and services. You also can check on businesses by calling the local Better Business Bureau before you purchase a product or service. You work hard for your money, do not throw it away.

SCAMS AND FRAUD

☐ Money is a temptation for any thief. If you receive Social Security or certain other retirement payments, you can have them electronically deposited directly into your bank account. This eliminates the chance they will be taken from your mailbox. There is also the possibility you will be observed and mugged while taking a month's benefits to or from your bank. Once you have the money deposited with the bank, use cash as little as possible and never carry large amounts of cash. You may be able to pay some of your bills at the bank. Better yet, use a checking account to pay all your bills including groceries and other purchases as well. If you need to withdraw savings for a special purchase, receive the amount as a cashier's check from the bank, not in cash bills. Christmas shopping will take careful planning in advance.

❑ Do not give out your credit card numbers to unknown callers offering "special, limited-time deals." You may receive the merchandise you ordered, but it will scarcely resemble what was promised. Thoroughly check all businesses who contact you before you do business with them. If a firm must have your order today, take your business elsewhere.

❑ Use the same amount of caution with mail order companies as with other businesses. They may use phony sweepstakes, drawings, contests, prizes, anything to hook you. Some of these scams can be very convincing, so be careful. You may want to call the police, your state's Attorney General, or the Better Business Bureau before dealing with these offers or companies.

❑ If you discover a scam or fraud, report it immediately to the police. You can also alert a broadcast station about this situation to notify the rest of your community.

MONEY SWINDLING SCHEMES

"BUNCO"

There are many types of fraudulent activity, but "Bunco" is a specialized type of swindle. Two of the most obvious and most frequent Bunco schemes are:

"THE BANK EXAMINER"

A phony bank examiner contacts you and asks for your help in catching a dishonest bank employee. He or she asks you to withdraw a specified amount of cash from your account and turn it over to him so he can check the serial numbers. After turning over your money to the examiner, you never see it again. Banks never use this procedure, only con men do.

"THE PIGEON DROP"

This one accounts for about half of the con games reported to the police! The swindlers claim to have found a large sum of money and offer to "share" it with you. However, they request you withdraw "good faith" money from the bank. The swindlers take your good faith money, then make phony arrangements for you to collect your share of the "found" money. Obviously, you will never see your money ever again.

Do not turn over any money if you are contacted by someone using one of these schemes or something similar involving any amount of money. If possible, call the police promptly, so they can try to prevent these bunco artists from swindling the next person they contact.

JUST SAY "NO" TO BUNCO!

❏   Swindlers often will be well dressed, talkative and intelligent. These criminals normally do not deal in force. They are trying to win your confidence. Con artists will play on your natural inclination to be helpful and the opportunity to take advantage of a windfall.

❏   Always be highly suspicious of "get rich quick" and "sounds to good to be true" schemes. Pyramid and similar multi-level marketing programs have become especially popular in the last ten years. The only person to get rich quick is the person who now has your money instead of you. If you decide to "invest" in one of these, do not invest any more money than you can afford to throw away or lose.

❏   Citizens of all ages have problems with business practices which are misleading and deceptive. Senior citizens are frequently targets for a range of investment possibilities involving retirement living or retirement incomes. There is no magic way to get rich, so enter any investment program only after carefully checking all relevant factors. Talk to the people at your bank, other business advisors as you deem appropriate, and the Better Business Bureau or consumer affairs services in your community. The main thing to remember is not to act impulsively. If you take time to carefully plan your investments, chances are that you will not fall into swindles or other problem deals.

**   *Special Note:* "*White-Collar Crime 101 Prevention Handbook*" by Jane Y. Kusic is a book which goes into more detail about various kinds of frauds. A copy can be obtained by contacting White-Collar Crime 101, 8300 Boone Boulevard, Suite 500, Vienna, Virginia 22182, (703) 848-9248.

FIRE PROTECTION

Although fire protection is not actually crime related, the authors feel safety issues absolutely have a place in this book. Our goal in writing, "Women and Children First" is to keep you and your family safe and secure. With this intent in mind, we felt justified in incorporating the fire safety tips and fire protection information presented in the next few chapters.

Fire cannot only destroy all of your personal belongings, but can be equally destructive with human lives. It is very important to plan and take all of the necessary safety steps before a fire occurs. Make sure your fire insurance covers the **replacement value** of all items in your home. Make a detailed written and photographic, or video record, of everything you own. This information should be put in a safety deposit box. Keep your list updated semi-annually and immediately change it when you make major purchases.

❑ If you discover a fire, leave the building and sound the alarm. Know where the fire exits are located in every building you frequent. Call the emergency number which is usually listed on the phone or on the first page of the phone book.

❑ Put all emergency numbers and your address on all telephones.

❑ If you are in a burning building, go to the nearest exit or stairs. Do not use an elevator. Feel door handles. If they are hot, do not open the door. Try to exit through a window. If the exit is blocked, return to your room, close the door, open the window and call for help. Stay close to the floor to escape breathing the smoke.

❑ When staying in hotels/motels, always count the number of doors to the nearest exit. This way, you can locate these exits even if visibility is poor.

☐ If you are trapped in a burning structure, if available, place a wet towel or cloth under the door to prevent smoke from entering your room. Many travelers carry a small role of duct tape when they travel to tape over vents and door openings if they find themselves trapped in a burning room.

☐ Practice fire safety techniques and plans thoroughly with all family members or building residents.

☐ Learn and practice cardiopulmonary resuscitation (CPR). Most local fire departments sponsor free classes to area residents. The life you save could be that of someone you love.

☐ When you are in a room with a fire, be careful when opening the windows. This could feed the fire more oxygen and cause it to grow faster. If you are in a smoke filled room which does not contain fire, seal all gaps around doors, ventilation ducts, and other spaces before opening windows. Stay close to the floor in smoke inundated rooms since more breathable air is below the smoke and heat. Have an emergency escape plan worked out before a fire occurs.

☐ Never play or tamper with fire alarms or fire extinguishers. They could save your life. Have fire extinguishers tested and serviced every year. This is required by fire code. Make sure your apartment complexes and businesses strictly adhere to these regulations.

☐ Make sure your building or house complies with **current** fire and safety codes. It could save your life, or the life of someone you love. If you are not sure, have the local fire department survey your house or apartment building. A report on violations can be done anonymously.

☐ Read ALL the instructions on fire extinguishers in your home and work areas. Know what types of fire extinguishers are available and what types of fires they are used for. If a fire breaks out you will not have the time to read the instructions. The proper use of these life saving devices should be taught to all members of your family.

❑ Keep all potentially flammable materials away from combustible sources like furnaces and electrical wiring or boxes. Also, do not store volatile chemicals together. It may be extremely dangerous to mix various cleaning products containing bleach, ammonia, lye, acids, and phosphates. If certain combinations of these chemicals are mixed, they can explode and produce toxic fumes. Read all product labels carefully and thoroughly. If you have any questions about certain substances, contact your local fire department.

❑ If you have a burglar alarm system, get a smoke detector installed with your system. It is advisable to have the system monitored by an alarm monitoring company.

❑ Many fire departments distribute child or "tot" finders and pet locator decals. These should be placed on all windows of your home containing children and pets.

❑ Install smoke detectors in every major room of your home. The expense of installing smoke detectors is minimal compared to the loss you will suffer from an undetected fire.

❑ Consider installing natural gas detectors and carbon monoxide monitors in your home.

❑ For second story rooms, provide escape ladders and practice using them in fire drills.

❑ Purchase fire extinguishers for your home. The best type of home extinguisher is rated "A,B,C." This is a multi-purpose fire extinguisher which will fight wood, paper, fabric, plastic, grease, oil, gasoline and electrical fires. Look for equipment which is approved by the National Fire Protection Association (NFPA). According to fire code, the fire extinguishers should be checked, serviced, or replaced yearly. This is necessary since the gases in an extinguisher can escape over time, making it useless.

CHECK LIST FOR FIRE PROTECTION

✔ Never tamper or play with fire alarms or extinguishers.

✔ Practice fire safety techniques and escape routes, especially for young children.

✔ Make sure your building meets federal, state and local fire code. This can be determined through your local fire department.

✔ Learn and practice CPR.

✔ Carefully store all flammable materials.

✔ When you discover a fire, leave the building and sound an alarm.

✔ If the building is on fire, go to the nearest exit or fire escape.

✔ Do not use elevators.

✔ Do not open hot doors.

✔ Stay close to the ground in smoke filled rooms.

✔ Have all items recorded for an insurance inventory. Make sure your insurance covers these items at replacement value.

✔ Know how to use a fire extinguisher before a fire occurs.

✔ Teach all members of your family proper extinguishing procedures.

✔ Know the different classes of fire extinguishers and what types of fires they are used for.

HOME EVACUATION OR EXIT PLAN

You should have a home evacuation plan. If you have children, practice your exit or evacuation plan at least once a month. Practice at night since most fires occur between 8:00 p.m. and 8:00 a.m.

☐ Have a common outside meeting place for your family to gather in case of a fire. All family members should go to this area immediately after exiting the burning structure. With this procedure, you will be assured that all family members are safely out of the house. Many lives are lost because individuals return to a burning building believing it is still occupied. These tragedies could have been avoided with a common meeting area for building occupants.

☐ In case of a fire, crawl to an exit and feel the doors for heat before entering a room.

☐ When the fire department does respond to your area, keep your children away from emergency equipment and personnel.

☐ Try to identify two exit points for each room in the house or apartment.

☐ In case of fire, try to shut doors to delay the spread of flames.

☐ If you live in a multi-level structure, make sure there is a fire escape ladder. It must be installed correctly. Practice using it with all family members if it is possible and safe to do so. Explain to children this device is not a toy. It should be used in an emergency only.

❏ Know the correct procedure to open or break windows. If you are in an emergency situation, throw a heavy object through the window. Use a solid instrument to break away the remaining pieces of glass that pose a hazard. Generally, a chair will serve this purpose.

❏ Make sure children can easily open windows.

❏ Keep a whistle by every bed to alert family members of a fire.

❏ NEVER return to the house once it has been evacuated. Several household items will produce toxic fumes even in the absence of flames. Wait until the fire department allows you to enter. You and your family members are more important than any possessions you own.

THE TWO TYPES OF SMOKE DETECTORS

Ionization – The detector's sensor contains a minute amount of radioactivity that conducts electricity between two electrodes. When the initial particles of combustion disturb the flow between the electrodes, the alarm is activated. These detectors usually discover fires, before smoke particles are created, in an earlier stage of development than photoelectric-type detectors.

Photoelectric – This detector's sensor uses a photoelectric cell and a light source. When smoke particles block light reaching the photoelectric cell, the alarm is activated. Generally, smoke particles, as a by-product of combustion, trigger the detector to alarm. Photoelectric detectors have fewer false alarms in smoky, dusty, or humid environments than ionization detectors.

☐ Buy as many smoke detectors as you feel appropriate to adequately cover your home.

☐ Place a smoke detector in the sleeping areas of all occupants, especially those who smoke cigarettes.

☐ As previously mentioned, if your house is heated by natural gas, install gas detectors and smoke detectors. Both can save your life.

☐ Consider purchasing carbon monoxide monitors for integration into your security and fire protection system.

PLACEMENT OF SMOKE DETECTORS

☐ Place smoke detectors on ceilings at least eight to ten inches from walls. Heat pockets form in ceiling/wall corner areas. This may cause false alarms in your smoke/heat detectors.

☐ If you are going to install a smoke detector on a wall, mount it high, but at least eight to ten inches below the ceiling.

☐ Install smoke detectors at least three feet away from wall or ceiling vents.

☐ Only purchase fire detection equipment which is Underwriters Laboratories, Inc. (UL) tested and National Fire Prevention Association (NFPA) approved.

☐ Make sure the alarm is loud enough to awaken you.

☐ Smoke detectors should have a trouble signal which indicates when the batteries are low.

☐ Make sure there is a manufacturer's warranty. A good smoke/heat detector should have a warranty lasting at least five years.

☐ Smoke detectors should be easy to maintain and clean.

☐ If your home is heated by natural gas, install gas detectors in all locations containing pilot lights.

☐ Test your smoke detector's battery every month by depressing the alarm test button located on most alarms. It is recommended that you replace the battery and vacuum dust out of the smoke detector annually.

APPENDIX 1
SECURITY HARDWARE AND DEVICES

The hardware and devices listed in this section are suggested items which may help increase your personal, residential, and vehicular security. The authors give general product descriptions, price, installation difficultly, and where items can be found. There is no specific reference to brand names for most products except those which require mentioning for identification purposes. The mention of a product name or product supplier is not intended as an endorsement. These items are only suggested and their effectiveness changes with each criminal situation.

The authors suggest using extreme caution when purchasing any security item or device. As with many other products, you get what you pay for. Your local police department's crime prevention officer is an excellent resource for advice on these security items and availability in your area.

Residential

1.)   Installed/Hardwired Burglar Alarm System

Price: $100.00 – $1000.00 depending on whether
                            you purchase or lease the system.

Installation: Difficult and should be done by a licensed
                            professional so the system meets electrical
                            codes.

Availability: Most areas have alarm companies. Contact
                            several companies for comparisons if
                            possible.

2.)   Underline: Wireless Burglar Alarm Systems

Price: $150.00—$1000.00

Installation: Moderately easy to difficult depending on the
                      system. Some basic systems can be installed
                      by yourself while others require licensed
                      professionals.

Availability: Some hardware stores, large chain
                      "everything" stores, and burglar alarm
                      companies.

Special Note: Wireless burglar alarm systems are prone to
                      more false alarms than hardwired systems.
                      Wireless systems have the tendency to pick
                      up random radio frequency signals which
                      cause the systems to trigger false alarms. The
                      sensors in these systems require batteries
                      which must be replaced periodically. Low
                      batteries may also trigger false alarms. This is
                      not to suggest all wireless systems are
                      ineffective, just that they have certain
                      characteristics.

3.)   Smoke/Heat Detectors

Price: $14.00—$21.00

Installation: Moderately easy.

Availability: Most hardware stores, large chain "everything"
                      stores, and burglar alarm companies .

4.)   Fire Escape Ladder (Two−story)

Price: $60.00−$75.00

Installation: Easy

Availability: Most hardware stores, large chain "everything" stores, and burglar alarm companies.

5.)   Fire Extinguishers ("A,B,C" Rated)

Price: $16.00−$48.00 depending on size.

Installation: None required.

Availability: Most hardware stores, large chain "everything" stores, and burglar alarm companies.

6.)   Deadbolt Locks

Price: Single deadbolt assembly − $15.00−$30.00. Combination deadbolt and locking door knob assembly − $32.00−$45.00.

Installation: Moderately difficult.

Availability: Almost all hardware stores and locksmith shops.

7.)   Strike Plates and Door Lock Reinforcement Kits

Price: $5.00−$20.00

Installation: Moderately difficult and should be done at the same time as the deadbolt.

Availability: Almost all hardware stores and locksmith shops .

8.)   Metal Dowels or Rods for the Tracks of Sliding Doors and Windows

Price: $2.00 – $5.00 for 36 inches of 3/8" – 5/8" metal material.

Installation: Easy

Availability: Most hardware stores.

9.)   Peepholes for Doors

Price: $6.00 – $9.00

Installation: Moderately difficult.

Availability: Almost all hardware stores and locksmith shops.

10.)   Sliding Door or Charlie Bar

Price: $15.00 – $20.00

Installation: Moderately easy.

Availability: Almost all hardware stores and locksmith shops.

11.)   Anti-Lift Sliding Door Shims

Price: $2.00 – $4.00

Installation: Easy

Availability: Almost all hardware stores and locksmith shops .

12.)   Window Locks

Price: Key operated locks — $5.00—$8.00. Pin-
                                   inserted or screw—tightened locks —
                                   $2.00—$5.00.

Installation: Easy

Availability: Almost all hardware stores and locksmith
                                   shops.

13.)   Exterior Motion Detecting Lights

Price: $12.00—$32.00

Installation: Moderately easy.

Availability: Most hardware and lighting stores.

14.)   Interior Motion Detecting Light Switches

Price: $8.00—$35.00

Installation: Moderately easy.

Availability: Most hardware and lighting stores .

PERSONAL DEVICES

1.)   Cayenne Pepper Concentrate Protection Spray

Price: $15.00 – $25.00 depending on size and type
                       of dispenser.

Availability: Limited. It can be found in certain mail order
                       catalogs and police equipment suppliers.
                       Remember to check with your state, county,
                       and city for regulations governing the use of
                       this substance. Do not violate any of these
                       regulations.

2.)   Portable/Wireless Motion Detectors for Travelling

Price: $49.00 – 69.00

Installation: None required.

Availability: "Damark International, Inc." mail order catalog,
                       1-800-729-9000. Damark has a continually
                       changing product line and catalog. This
                       product may or may not be available at the
                       present time. You should call the above
                       number for a current product catalog.

3.)   Police-Style or "Rape" Whistle

Price: $5.00 – 15.00

Special Note: You should buy a whistle which is durable
                       (stainless steel) and loud. Try to find one with
                       a distinctive pitch if possible. A distinctive
                       pitch or sound could potentially attract
                       attention sooner.

Availability: Police uniform stores or catalogs, variety
                       stores, and athletic supply stores .

VEHICLE ALARM SYSTEMS

1.)   Portable Vehicle Alarms

Price:	$50.00–$80.00.
Installation:	Easy.
Availability:	Some auto parts stores, auto speciality stores, large chain "everything" stores, "Damark International, Inc." mail order catalog, 1-800-729-9000. Damark has a continually changing product line and catalog. This product may or may not be available at the present time. You should call the above number for a current product catalog.

2.)   Installed/Hardwired Vehicle Alarm Systems

Price:	$250.00–$500.00
Installation:	Professionally installed.
Availability:	Limited to auto speciality store dealers and car dealerships.

There are several catalog companies which also offer vehicle alarms and safety devices. Contact the two companies listed on the following page for a current catalog. The authors do not endorse or guarantee the quality or availability of these companies' products. They are listed as an informational resource only.

☐ "Crutchfield" mail order catalog, 1-800-336-5566. Crutchfield offers car alarms and a home security system along with many other electronic entertainment products. These various security products may or may not be available at the present time. You can call the above number for a current product catalog.

☐ "J.C. Whitney & Co." — mail order catalog, 1-312-431-6102. J.C. Whitney & Co. specializes in automotive parts and products including vehicle alarms. These various security products may or may not be available at the present time. You can call the above number for a current product catalog.

OTHER SOURCES FOR SECURITY PRODUCTS

The companies listed below offer a variety of security products in their catalogs. If you are interested, you can call these companies and request a catalog. All of these companies do not necessarily specialize in security products, but offer some security related items throughout their product lines. The authors do not endorse or guarantee the quality or availability of these companies' products. *These companies are listed as an informational resource only.*

1.)   *"Damark International, Inc."* mail order catalog, 1-800-729-9000. Damark has a continually changing product line and catalog. Various security products may or may not be available at the present time. You can call the above number for a current product catalog.

2.)   *"DAK Industries, Inc."* mail order catalog, 1-800-325-0800. DAK has a continually changing product line and catalog. Various security products may or may not be available at the present time. You can call the above number for a current product catalog.

3.)   *"Secure-1 Network"* allows you to become a member of their network for a fee. This membership generally consists of a newsletter and videotape featuring various security products which have been mentioned throughout this book. The "Secure-1 Network" product line are security related products. You can call 1-800-732-0299 for complete and updated information.

APPENDIX 2
ADDITIONAL READING

The books listed in this section present a wide variety of techniques and options for crime prevention. It is best to read through these books, compare information, and decide which strategies work best for your particular circumstances. These books go into more detail about specific criminal environments than does *"Women and Children First: How to AVOID Crime."* However, *"Women and Children First: How to AVOID Crime"* is designed to provide quick and easy to remember crime avoidance techniques. The authors do not personally endorse any of the books in this section or their advice since each crime has its own unique characteristics.

Title: *The Sixth Sense: Practical Tips for Everyday Safety*

Author: Joseph Niehaus

Publisher: Blue Bird Publishing, Tempe, AZ
Copyright 1990

Title: *The Complete Guide to Home Security: How to Protect Your Family and Home From Harm.*

Author: David Alan Wacker

Publisher: Betterway Publications, White Hall, VA
Copyright 1990

Title: *How to Protect Yourself from Crime*

Author: I. A. Lipman

Publisher: Atheneum, SMI, New York, NY
Copyright 1975, 1984, 1989

Title: *Safe & Sound: A Parents Guide on Self-protection for Kids.*

Authors: E. Gordon Franks & Susan Erling

Publisher: Safe & Sound Productions, Golden Valley, MN
Copyright 1990

Title: *Home Security — Consumer Reports Books*

Authors: Sydney C. Cooper, Anne Scott, and the Editors of Consumer Reports Books

Publisher: Consumers Union, Mount Vernon, NY
Copyright 1988

Title: *Ray Johnson's Total Security*

Authors: Ray Johnson with Carroll Stoianoff

Publisher: New American Library, New York, NY
Copyright 1985

Title: *Keeping Out Of Crime's Way — An AARP Book*

Authors: J.E. Persico with George Sunderland

Publisher: Scott, Foresman and Company, Glenview, Illinois and the American Association of Retired Persons (AARP), Washington, D.C.

Title: *Help Kids Say No to Drugs and Drinking: A Practical Prevention Guide for Parents*

Author: Bob Schroeder

Publisher: CompCare Publishers, Minneapolis, MN
Copyright 1987

Title:	*Security for Senior Citizens: How to Make the Golden Years Safer*
Author:	David Y. Coverston
Publisher:	Security Seminars Press, Ocala, FL Copyright 1988

APPENDIX 3
ASSAILANT DESCRIPTION RECORD

The following information should be completed as soon as possible following a criminal incident. It is much easier to remember and record the details right after the crime has just occurred rather than relying on your memory later. By recording this information immediately, it will also help you to remember details later if it becomes necessary to testify in court.

The publisher gives permission to duplicate all forms in Appendix 3 through 9. It is recommended you make several copies of the Appendix sections for future use.

CRIMINAL INCIDENT DESCRIPTION RECORD

DATE: TIME OF   TYPE OF
                 INCIDENT: INCIDENT:

NUMBER OF INDIVIDUALS INVOLVED:

            VICTIM(S):   PERPETRATOR(S):   AGE(S):
MALE(S):
FEMALE(S):

NAMES: HEIGHT: WEIGHT: VICTIM: PERP:
1. _____ _____ _____ _____ _____
2. _____ _____ _____ _____ _____
3. _____ _____ _____ _____ _____
4. _____ _____ _____ _____ _____
5. _____ _____ _____ _____ _____

    AGE: SEX: ADDRESS: PHONE:

1. _____ _____ _____ _____
2. _____ _____ _____ _____
3. _____ _____ _____ _____
4. _____ _____ _____ _____
5. _____ _____ _____ _____

COMMENTS:

PHYSICAL CHARACTERISTICS — PERPETRATOR

SLIGHT BUILD: Y/N
MEDIUM BUILD: Y/N
HEAVY BUILD: Y/N

NOTICEABLE SCARS, MARKS, OR TATTOOS: Y/N
DESCRIBE:

FACE:

   THIN   FAT   MUSTACHE: Y/N
   ROUND ANGULAR   BEARD: Y/N

BREATH:

   ALCOHOL PRESENT: Y/N

VOICE:

   CALM: Y/N
   NERVOUS: Y/N
   LOW PITCH: Y/N
   HIGH PITCH: Y/N

COMPLEXION: (CIRCLE)

DARK   LIGHT   RUDDY   PALE

HAIR: COLOR: _____

   THICK   THIN   STRAIGHT   CURLY

   HAIR PART LOCATION: _____
   STYLE OF COMBING: _____

EYES: COLOR: _____

   FAR APART   CLOSE TOGETHER
   SMALL   LARGE

NOSE:

LARGE	SMALL	
NARROW	FAT	
SHORT	LONG	

CHIN:

SQUARE	ROUNDED (FAT)
NARROW	LONG
SHORT	

EARS:

LARGE	SMALL
CLOSE TO HEAD	EXTENDED

CLOTHING

HAT: Y/N

                COLOR:
                STYLE:
                CONDITION:

COAT OR JACKET:

      COLOR:_____
      STYLE:_____
      TYPE:_____
      CONDITION:_____
      INSIGNIAS:_____

TIE:

      COLOR:_____
      STYLE:_____
      TYPE:_____
      CONDITION:_____
      INSIGNIAS:_____

SHIRT:
        COLOR:_____
        STYLE:_____
        TYPE:_____
        CONDITION:_____
        INSIGNIAS:_____

PANTS:
        COLOR:_____
        STYLE:_____
        TYPE:_____
        CONDITION:_____
        INSIGNIAS:_____

GLOVES:
        COLOR:_____
        STYLE:_____
        TYPE:_____
        CONDITION:_____

SOCKS:
        COLOR:_____

SHOES:
        COLOR:_____
        STYLE:_____
        TYPE:_____
        CONDITION:_____
        INSIGNIAS:_____
        BRAND:_____

JEWELRY:
        DESCRIBE:

APPENDIX 4
AUTOMOBILE DESCRIPTION

The Automobile Description record should be copied and completed for each vehicle you own. This information should be placed in a safe deposit box or in your "safe records area" for retrieval if your car is stolen.

AUTOMOBILE DESCRIPTION — YOUR VEHICLE
YEAR:
MAKE:
MODEL:
LICENSE NUMBER:
VEHICLE IDENTIFICATION NUMBER:
COLOR:
BODY STYLE: (NUMBER OF DOORS):
SHAPE OF   TAILLIGHTS:
NUMBER AND SHAPE   OF HEADLIGHTS:
DENTS OR BLEMISHES:
BUMPER STICKERS:
TIRE TYPE AND BRAND:
OUTSTANDING FEATURES:
COMMENTS:

APPENDIX 5
POLICE REPORT INFORMATION

Complete the following information immediately after any criminal report or incident. This information will help you track your case as it goes through the investigative, and later, court processes.

POLICE REPORT INFORMATION
TIME YOU NOTIFIED POLICE:
TIME THE POLICE OFFICER RECEIVED THE CALL (ASK THE OFFICER):
TIME THE POLICE OFFICER ARRIVED:
NAME OF OFFICER TAKING THE REPORT (ASK FOR A CARD):
NAME OF DEPARTMENT TAKING REPORT:
REPORT NUMBER:
PROCEDURES TO OBTAIN A COPY OF REPORT (ASK):
COMMENTS:

APPENDIX 6
AUTOMOBILE ACCIDENT REPORT

The following information should be carried in your car and completed immediately after an accident. Record the following information at the scene of the accident then review it for completeness the following day. This process may also help you to recall small details if you are called to testify in court.

AUTOMOBILE ACCIDENT REPORT

VEHICLE DRIVER — YOURS

NAME:_____

ADDRESS:_____

PHONE NUMBER:_____

VEHICLE DRIVER — THEIRS

NAME:_____

ADDRESS:_____

PHONE NUMBER:_____

DRIVERS LICENSE NUMBER:_____

INSURANCE COMPANY:_____

POLICY NUMBER:_____

VEHICLE PASSENGER — YOURS

NAME:_____

ADDRESS:_____

PHONE NUMBER: _____

LOCATION:_____

VEHICLE PASSENGER — YOURS

NAME:_____

ADDRESS:_____

PHONE NUMBER: _____

LOCATION:_____

VEHICLE PASSENGER – YOURS

NAME:_____

ADDRESS:_____

_____

PHONE NUMBER:_____

LOCATION:_____

VEHICLE PASSENGER – THEIRS

NAME:_____

ADDRESS:_____

_____

PHONE NUMBER:_____

LOCATION:_____

VEHICLE PASSENGER – THEIRS

NAME:_____

ADDRESS:_____

_____

PHONE NUMBER:_____

LOCATION:_____

VEHICLE PASSENGER – THEIRS

NAME:_____

ADDRESS:_____

_____

PHONE NUMBER:_____

LOCATION:_____

VEHICLE PASSENGER – THEIRS

NAME:_____

ADDRESS:_____

_____

PHONE NUMBER:_____

LOCATION:_____

WITNESS INFORMATION:

NAME:_____

ADDRESS:_____

_____

PHONE NUMBER:_____

LOCATION DURING ACCIDENT:_____

_____

_____

NAME OF WITNESS:

NAME:_____

ADDRESS:_____

_____

PHONE NUMBER:_____

LOCATION DURING ACCIDENT:_____

_____

_____

NAME OF WITNESS:

NAME:_____

ADDRESS:_____

_____

PHONE NUMBER:_____

LOCATION DURING ACCIDENT:_____

_____

_____

NAME OF WITNESS:

NAME:_____

ADDRESS:_____

_____

PHONE NUMBER:_____

LOCATION DURING ACCIDENT:_____

_____

_____

NAMES OF WITNESS:

NAME:_____

ADDRESS:_____

PHONE NUMBER:_____

LOCATION DURING ACCIDENT:_____

_____

_____

NAMES OF WITNESS:

NAME:_____

ADDRESS:_____

PHONE NUMBER:_____

LOCATION DURING ACCIDENT:_____

_____

_____

NAMES OF WITNESS:

NAME:_____

ADDRESS:_____

PHONE NUMBER:_____

LOCATION DURING ACCIDENT:_____

_____

_____

NAMES OF WITNESS:

NAME:_____

ADDRESS:_____

PHONE NUMBER:_____

LOCATION DURING ACCIDENT:_____

_____

_____

LOCATION OF THE ACCIDENT
BRIEF DESCRIPTION OF ACCIDENT:
TIME:
LOCATION:
CROSS ROAD: MILE MARKER:
DIRECTION OF TRAFFIC LANES: NORTH   SOUTH   EAST   WEST
DISTANCE FROM FIXED POINTS:
WEATHER CONDITIONS:
VISIBILITY OF AREA:
OBSTRUCTIONS TO VIEW OF AREA:

LIGHTING:

QUALITY OF
ROAD SURFACE:

TRAFFIC SIGNALS:

SPEED OF VEHICLES:
YOURS:
THEIRS:

COMMENTS:

VEHICLES INVOLVED IN ACCIDENT		
	1st VEHICLE	2nd VEHICLE
YEAR:		
MAKE:		
VEHICLE NUMBERS (VIN):		
COLOR:		
MILEAGE:		
OWNERSHIP:		
REGISTRATION:		
INSURANCE AND TYPE OF COVERAGE:		
WAS ALCOHOL INVOLVED?		
INJURIES TO VEHICLE OPERATORS:		
INJURIES TO PASSENGERS:		

INJURIES TO
PEDESTRIANS:

DEFECTS OR DAMAGE
TO YOUR VEHICLE
BEFORE ACCIDENT:

LIST ANY EMERGENCY
VEHICLES THAT RESPONDED:

ESTIMATE DAMAGE
TO ALL VEHICLES:

COMMENTS:

WOMEN AND CHILDREN FIRST:

In the event of an accident, you should fill out and give the information listed on this form to all parties involved. You may want to have this section completed before an accident.

INSURANCE INFORMATION
YOUR NAME:
WORK PHONE:
INSURANCE COMPANY:
POLICY NUMBER:
INSURANCE AGENT:
YOUR VEHICLE'S DESCRIPTION
MAKE:
MODEL:
YEAR:
COLOR:
V.I.N. NUMBER:
LICENSE NUMBER & STATE:

APPENDIX 7
SECURITY TRAVEL GUIDE

The information listed below should be completed before you leave on your trip. This may prevent you from getting lost, and in an emergency, aid you in reaching the desired emergency care provider.

HOTEL INFORMATION
HOTEL NAME:
PHONE:
ADDRESS:
MAJOR CROSS STREETS:
DIRECTIONS FROM FREEWAYS OR LANDMARKS:
DIRECTIONS TO NEAREST HOSPITAL:

HOSPITAL PHONE:

HOSPITAL ADDRESS:

DIRECTIONS TO   *
NEAREST POLICE
DEPARTMENT:

POLICE PHONE: *

POLICE ADDRESS: *

OTHER IMPORTANT PHONE NUMBERS:

_____   _____
_____   _____
_____   _____
_____   _____
_____   _____
_____   _____
_____   _____
_____   _____
_____   _____

*   Find out if the responding agency is from the state, county, or city jurisdictions.

APPENDIX 8
WOMEN'S TRAVEL LOG

This travel log is designed for your information. It is also intended to be furnished to a trusted friend for disclosure, in case of an emergency.

DESTINATION:	
WHO YOU ARE VISITING:	
ADDRESS:	
PHONE:	
DIRECTIONS FROM HOTEL:	
TIME OF ARRIVAL:	
TIME OF DEPARTURE:	
IN CASE OF EMERGENCY, CONTACT:	
NAME:	
PHONE:	
ADDRESS:	

PERSONAL INFORMATION
PHYSICAL DESCRIPTION:
HEIGHT:
WEIGHT:
HAIR COLOR:
EYE COLOR AND SHAPE:
SCARS OR DISTINGUISHABLE MARKS:
CLOTHES WORN TODAY:
COMMENTS:

APPENDIX 9
CHILD IDENTIFICATION PROFILE

CHILD'S FULL NAME:

NICK NAMES:

DATE OF BIRTH:

SEX: BLOOD TYPE:

COMMONLY TAKEN DRUGS:

SCHOOL NAME:

SCHOOL ADDRESS:

NAMES OF SCHOOL OFFICIALS:

CLASS SCHEDULE:

SPECIAL ACTIVITIES AND SCHEDULES:

NEIGHBORHOOD FRIENDS:

NAMES	PHONE NUMBERS	PARENTS NAMES	ADDRESS
_____	_____	_____	_____
_____	_____	_____	_____
_____	_____	_____	_____
_____	_____	_____	_____
_____	_____	_____	_____

ATTACH THE FOLLOWING TO YOUR CHILD'S INFORMATIONAL PROFILE:

SAMPLE OF CURRENT HANDWRITING
WRITTEN PHYSICAL DESCRIPTION
    HAIR COLOR   COMPLEXION BIRTHMARKS
    SCARS   HEIGHT   WEIGHT
    (SEE APPENDIX 3 FOR DESCRIPTION EXAMPLE)

DENTAL RECORDS (X-RAYS)
FINGER PRINTS
PALM PRINTS
TAPE A PIECE OF HAIR
INCLUDE A FINGERNAIL CLIPPING
COPIES OF AT LEAST 8 COLOR PHOTOGRAPHS
    (THIS SAVES DUPLICATION TIME)

DESCRIPTION OF BICYCLE:

COMMENTS:

(This page left intentially blank)

BIBLIOGRAPHY / INFORMATION SOURCES

American Association of Retired
Persons
1909 K Street N.W.
Washington, DC 20049
(202) 728-4363

Bellevue Police Department
Bellevue, Washington

Boise Neighborhood Watch Program
Boise Police Crime Prevention Office

California Council on Criminal Justice
Selected Crime Prevention Programs in
California
(Sacramento: California Council on
Criminal Justice, 1973)

Crime Prevention Assoc. of Oregon

Department of the Air Force
United States of America

"Don't Give a Thief A Free Ride,"
Metro Area Crime Prevention Round
Table, including:

    Beaverton Police Dept.
    Clackamas Co. Sheriff's Dept.
    Gresham Police Dept.
    Lake Oswego Police Dept.
    Multnomah Co. Sheriff's Dept.

Portland Police Dept.
Vancouver (WA) Dept.
Washington Co. Sheriffs Dept.
West Linn Police Dept.

Federal Bureau of Investigation's
Uniform Crime Reports for 1990

Idaho Crime Prevention Office
Law Enforcement Assistance Division
Department of Law Enforcement
6058 Corporal Lane
Boise, Idaho 83704

Idaho Department of Law Enforcement
Idaho Crime Prevention Office
6081 Clinton Street
Boise, Idaho 83704
(208) 334-2909

Institute of Criminal Justice Studies

Lakewood Department of Public Safety
Lakewood, Washington

Law Enforcement Assistance
Administration
United States Department of Justice

Maryland Crime Watch

Michigan Department of State Police
Crime Prevention Center

National Advisory Commission on
Criminal Justice Standards And Goals

National Automobile Theft Bureau

National Clearinghouse for Drug
Abuse Information
P.O. Box 416, Dept. DQ
Kensington, Maryland 20795

National Crime Prevention Council
805 15th Street, N.W.
Washington, DC 20005
(202) 393-7141

National Crime Prevention Institute

National Criminal Justice Reference
Service School Crime Desk
Box 6000
Rockville, Maryland 20850

National Fingerprint Center for Missing
Children
P.O. Box 945
Kirksville, Missouri 63501
(816) 627-1277

National Safety Council

Newark Police Department

North Carolina Domestic Violence
Project
526 N. Wilmington Street
Raleigh, North Carolina 27604
(919) 733-3455

Office of Justice Assistance,
Research, and Statistics
for the Crime Prevention Coalition

Parents and Youth Against Drug Abuse
(Idaho Drug Prevention)
P.O. Box 500
Boise, Idaho 83701

Sexual Assault and the Law
Moscow Police Department
Moscow, Idaho 83843

Crime Against Small Business
Small Business Administration
Washington, DC; U.S. Government
Printing Office, 1969

Small Business Administration
Report Numbers 209, No. 134,
No. 119

State Farm Fire and Casualty
Company
Bloomington, Illinois

Suburban Crime Prevention Unit
3161 Wilson Avenue S.W.
Grandville, Michigan 49418

The Crime Prevention Coalition

The Idaho Crime Prevention
Association
6113 Clinton Street
Boise, Idaho 83704
(208) 334-2909

WOMEN AND CHILDREN FIRST:

**The National Center for Missing and
Exploited Children**
1835 K Street N.W. Suite 700
Washington, DC 20006
(202) 634-9821.
1-800-843-5678
(If you know the location of a missing
child)

The National Sheriffs' Association

The Southland Corporation
2828 North Haskell Avenue
Dallas, TX 75221

**U.S. Department of Health And Human
Services**
Public Health Service
Alcohol, Drug Abuse, and Mental Health
Administration

INDEX